Art Designs for **Kids**

# GRAFFITI
## COLORING BOOKS

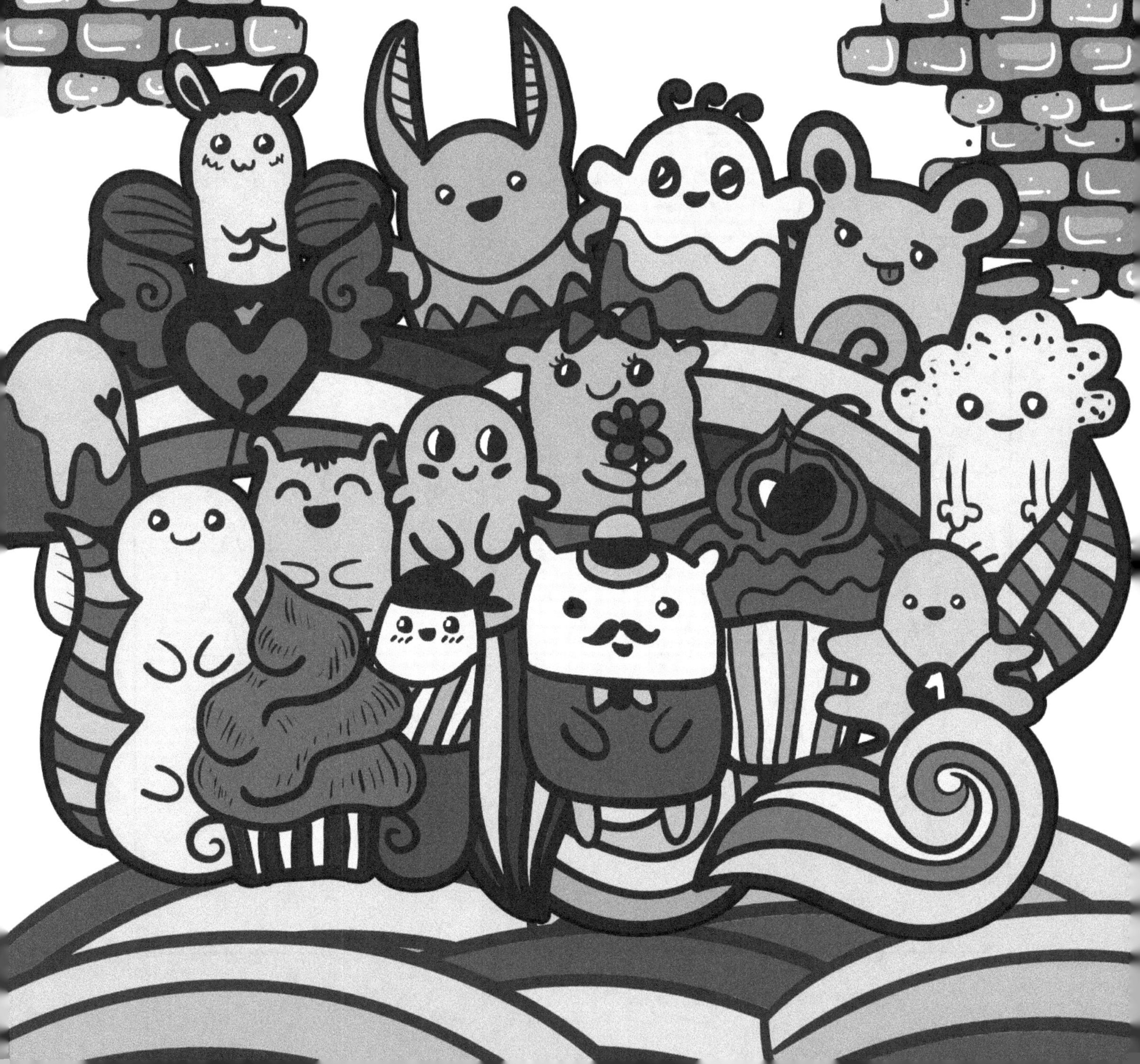

# TEST YOUR COLOR

# TEST YOUR COLOR

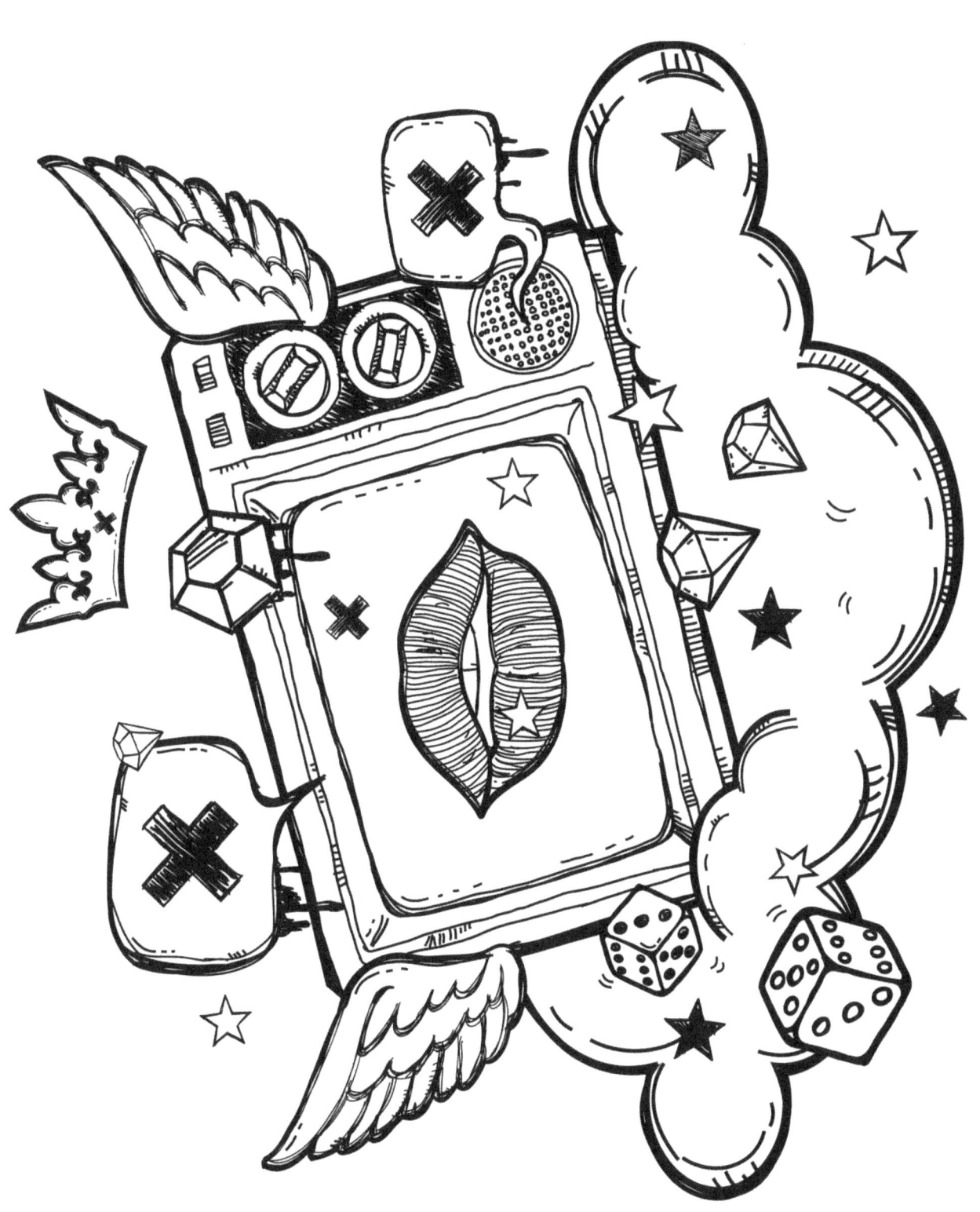

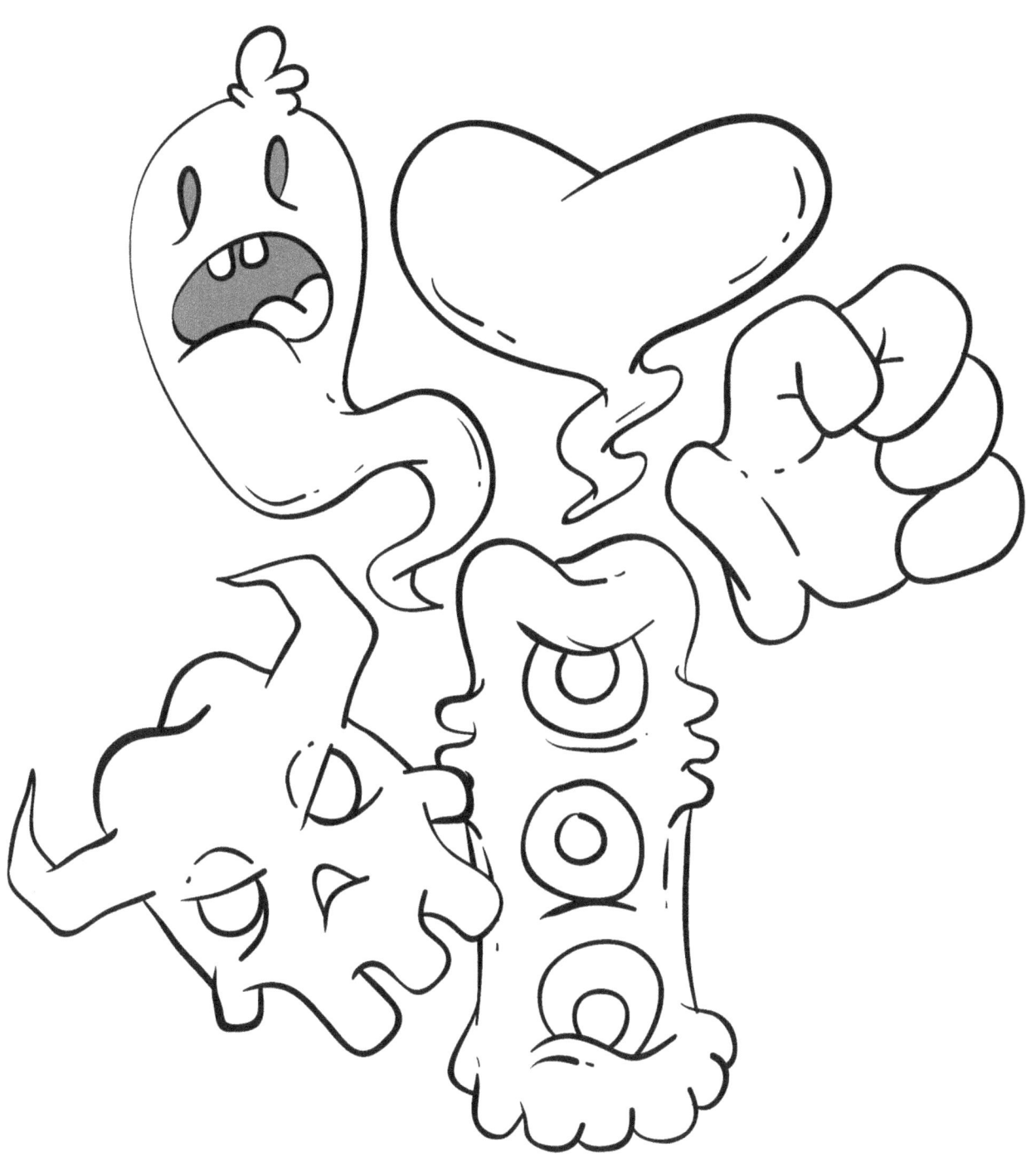

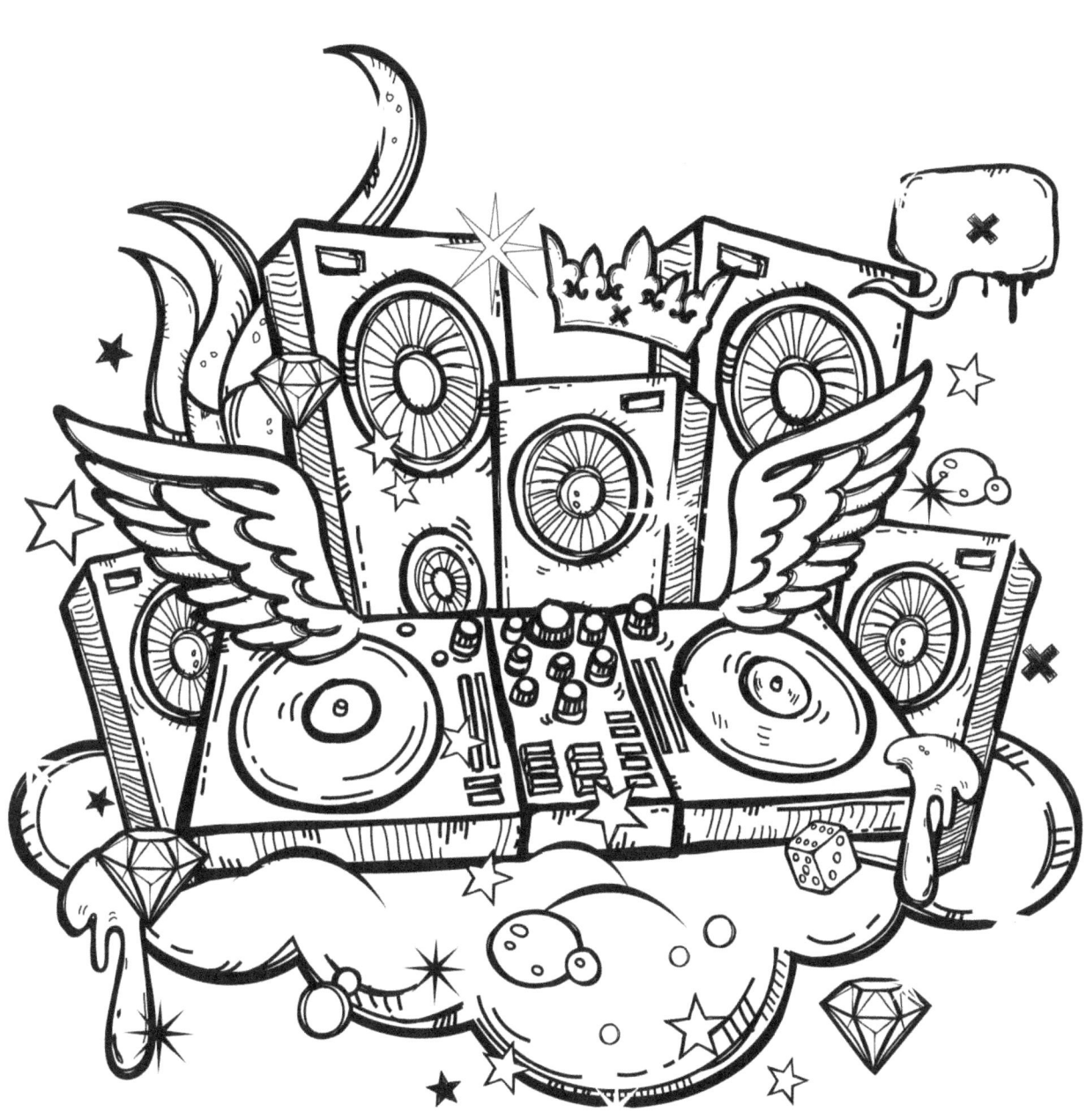

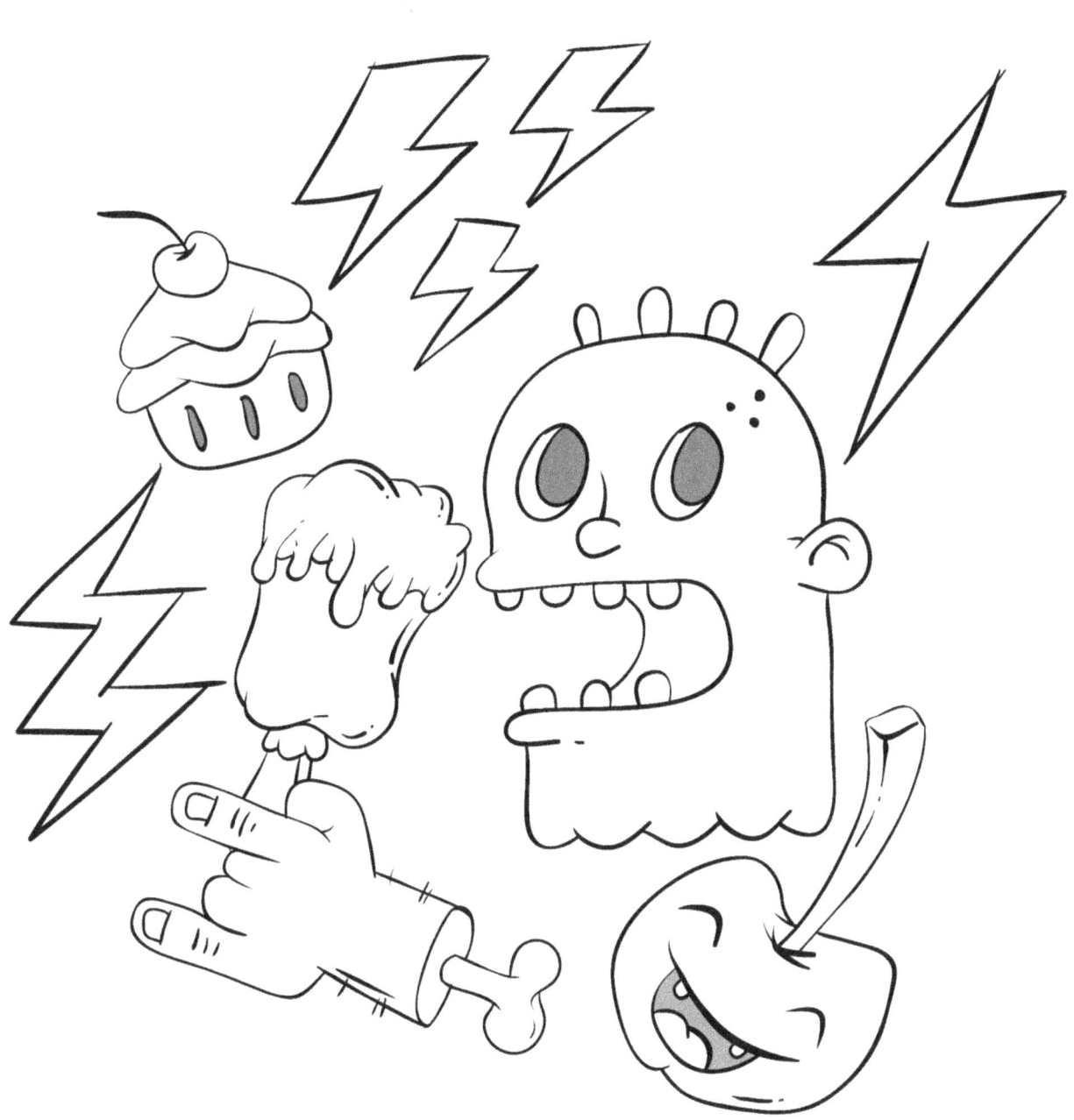

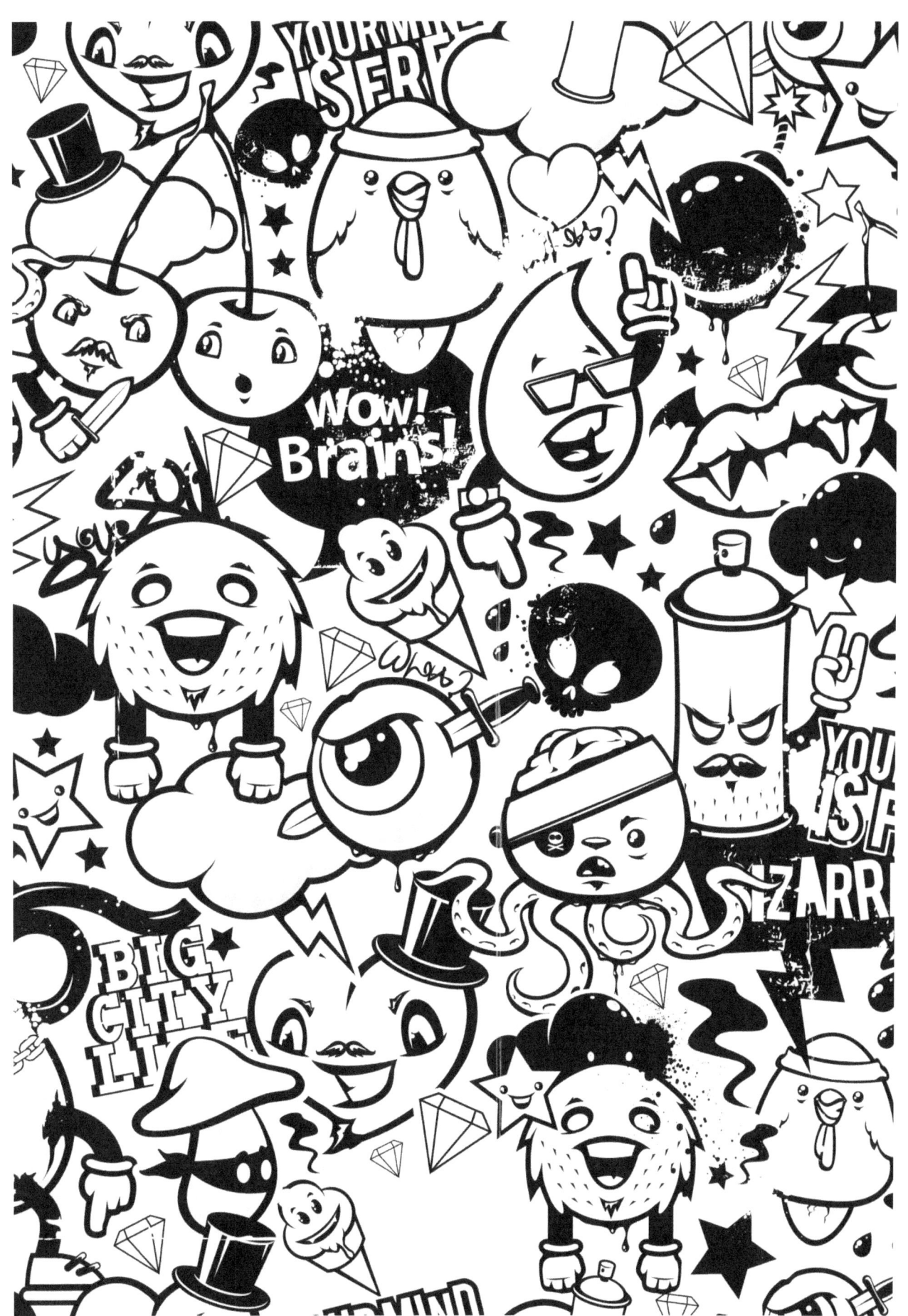

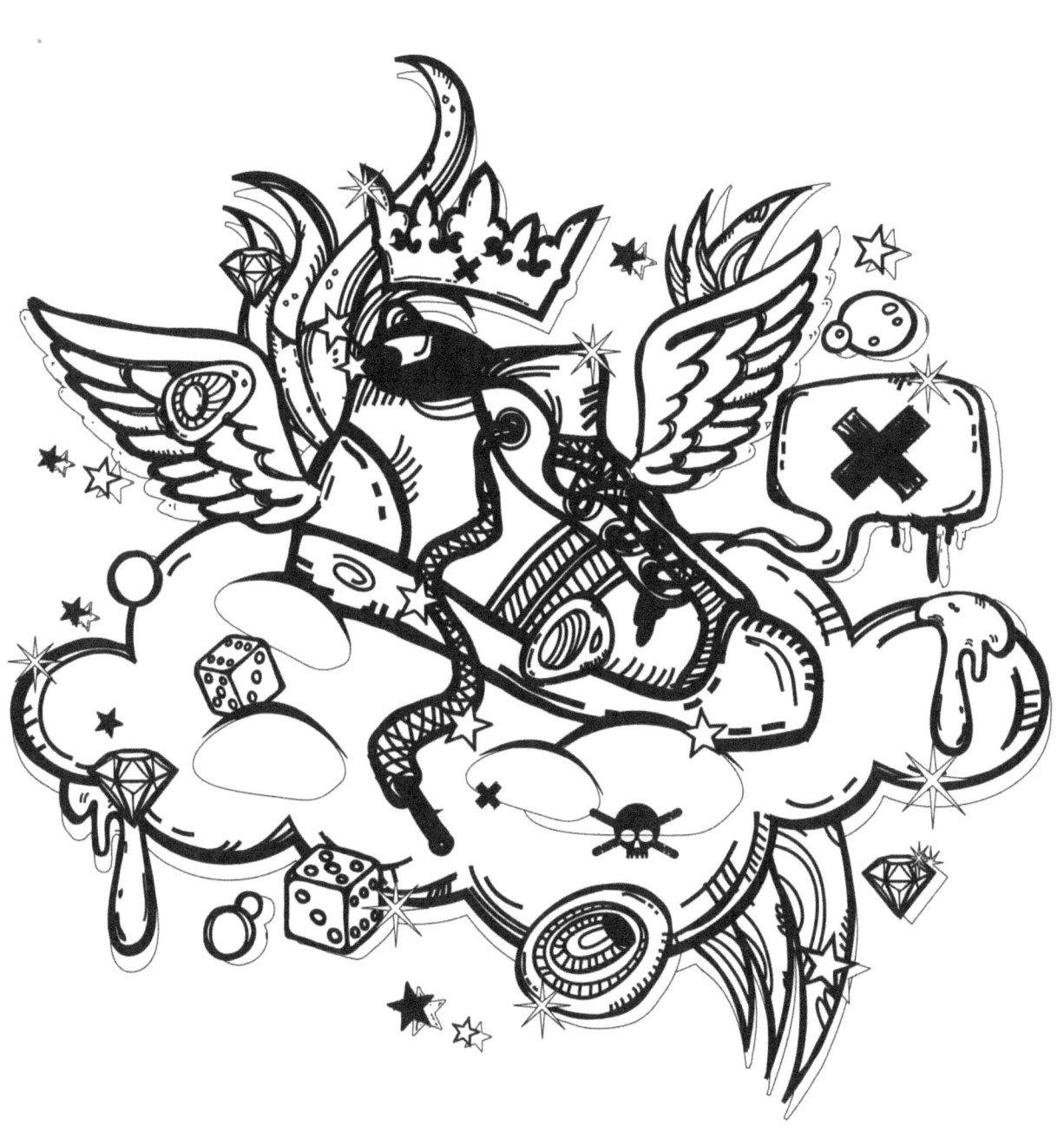

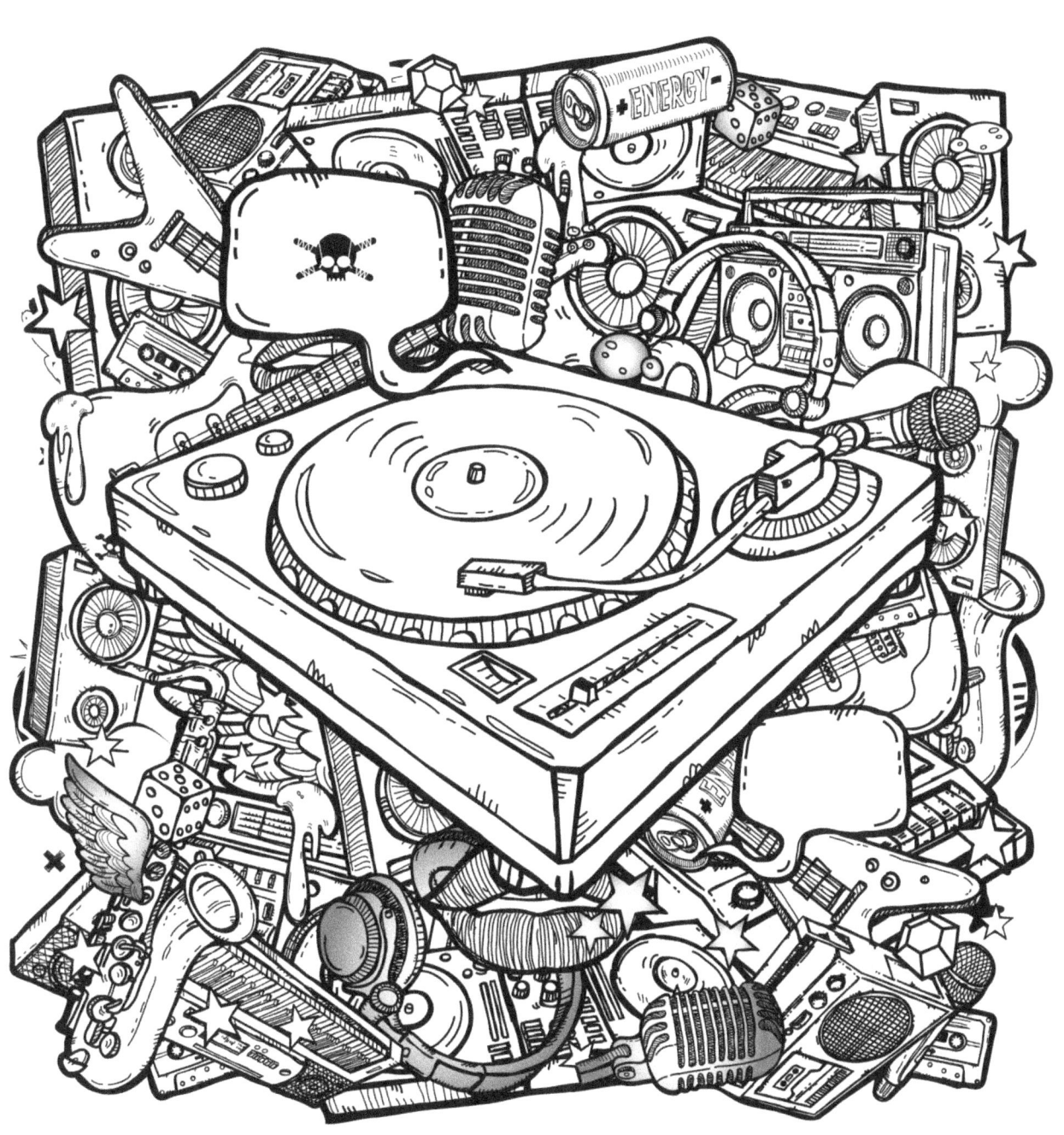

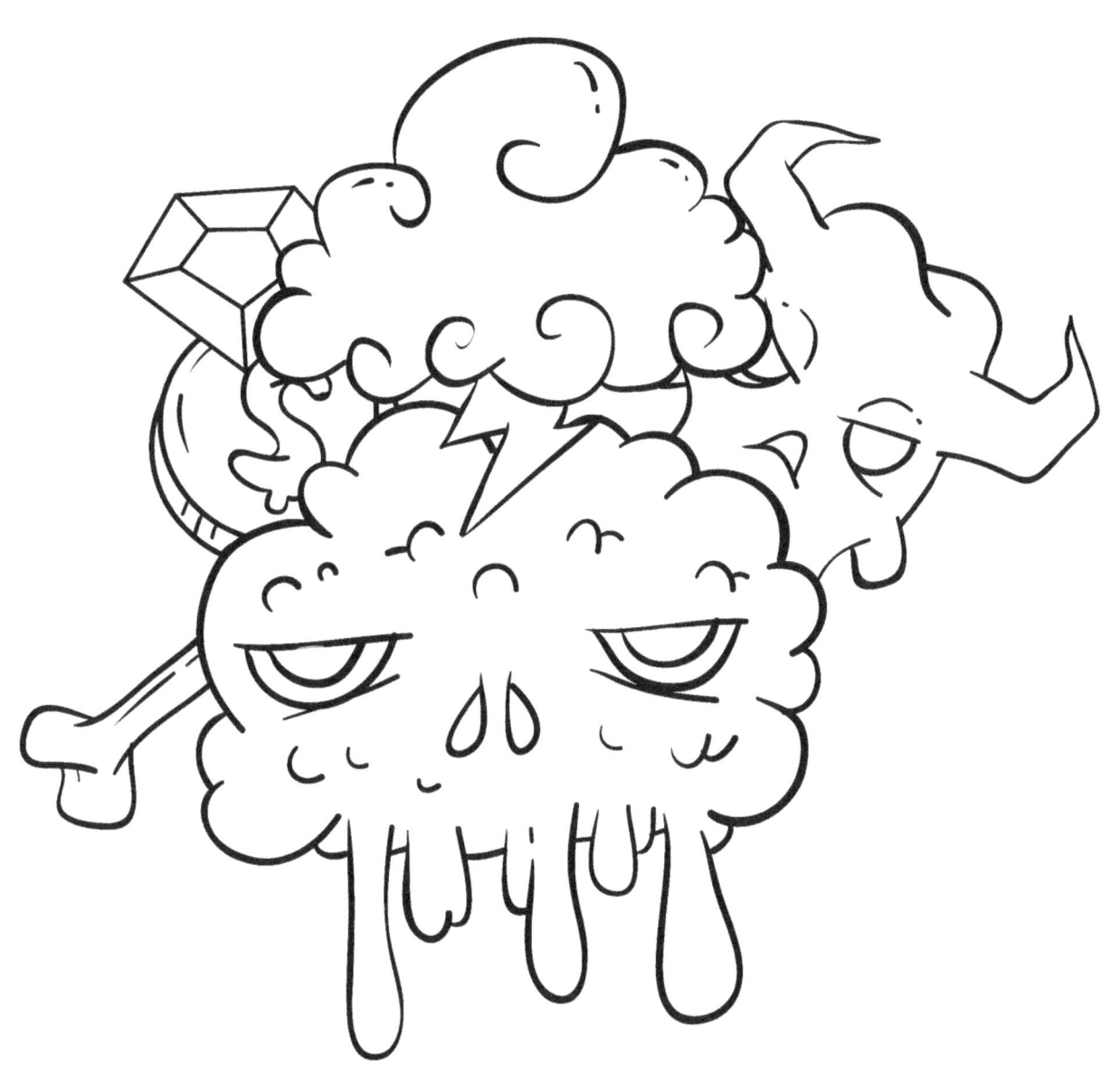

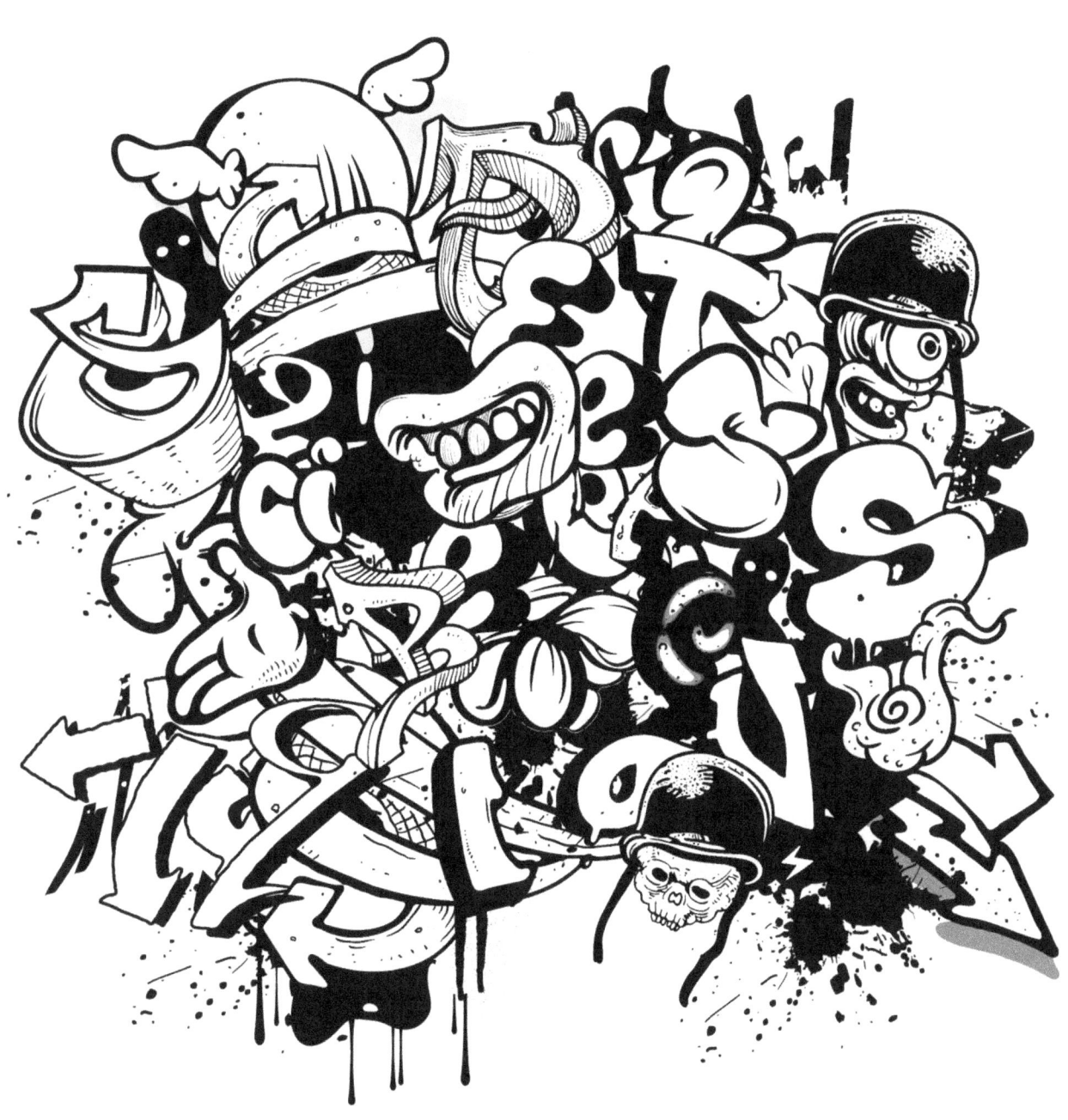

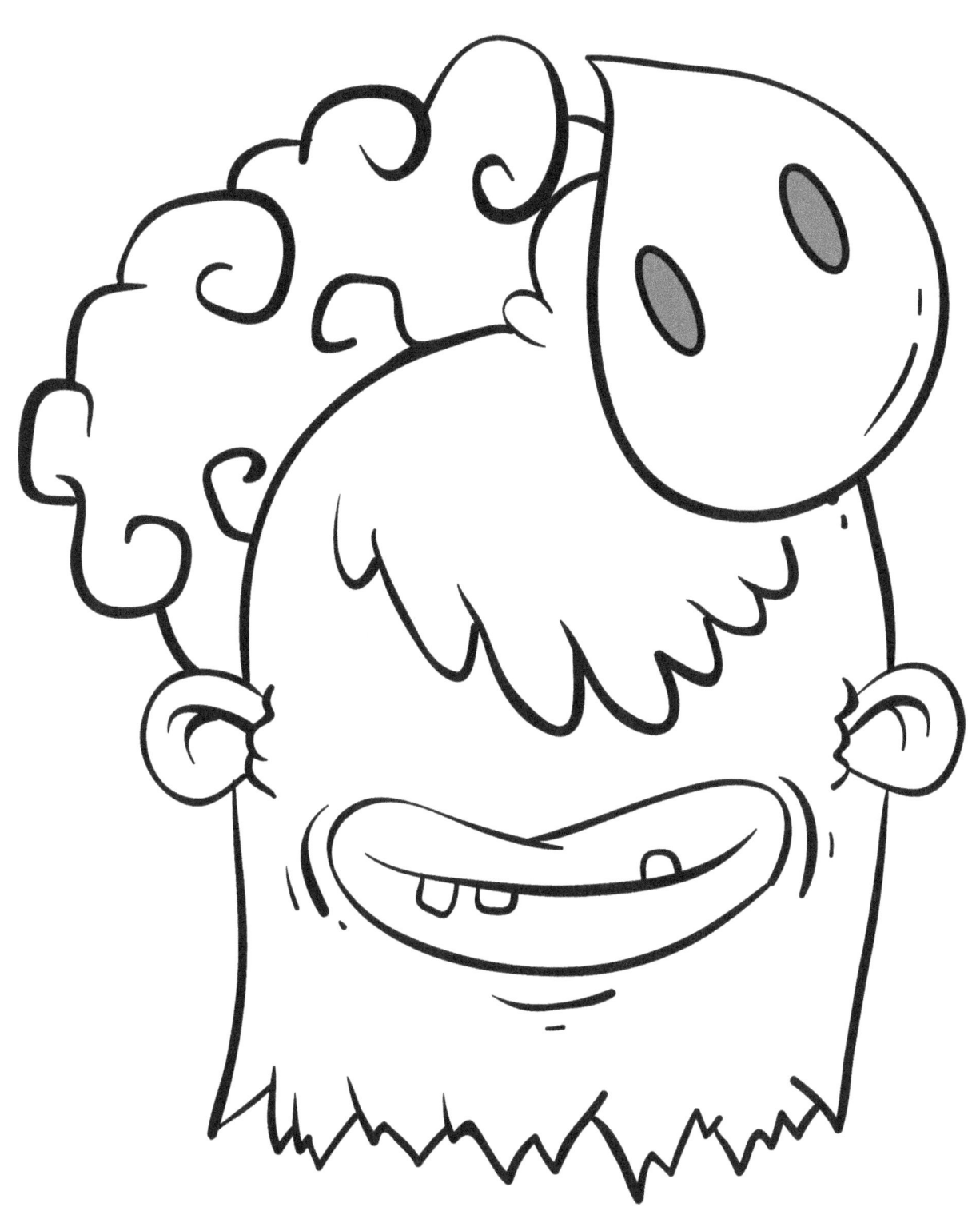

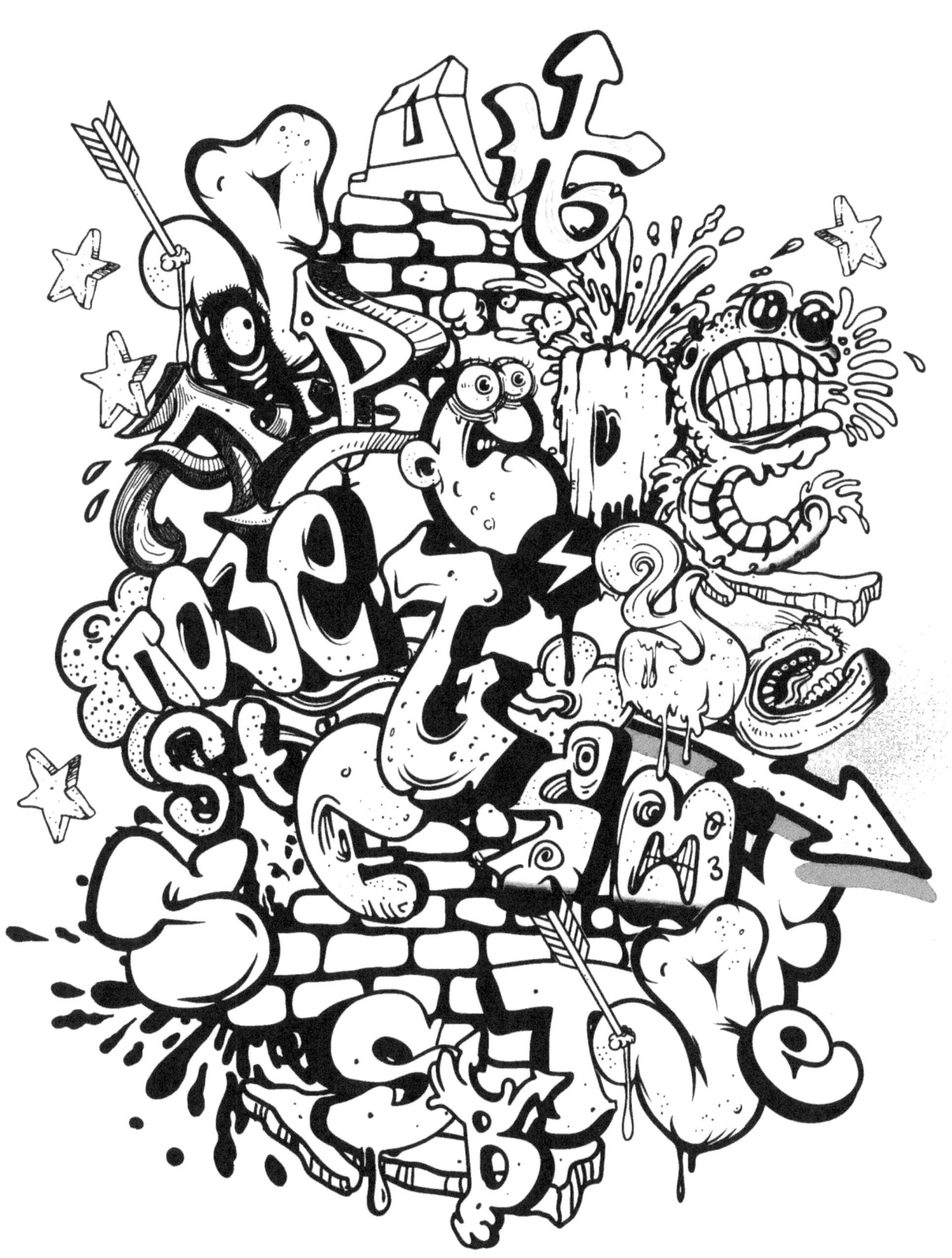

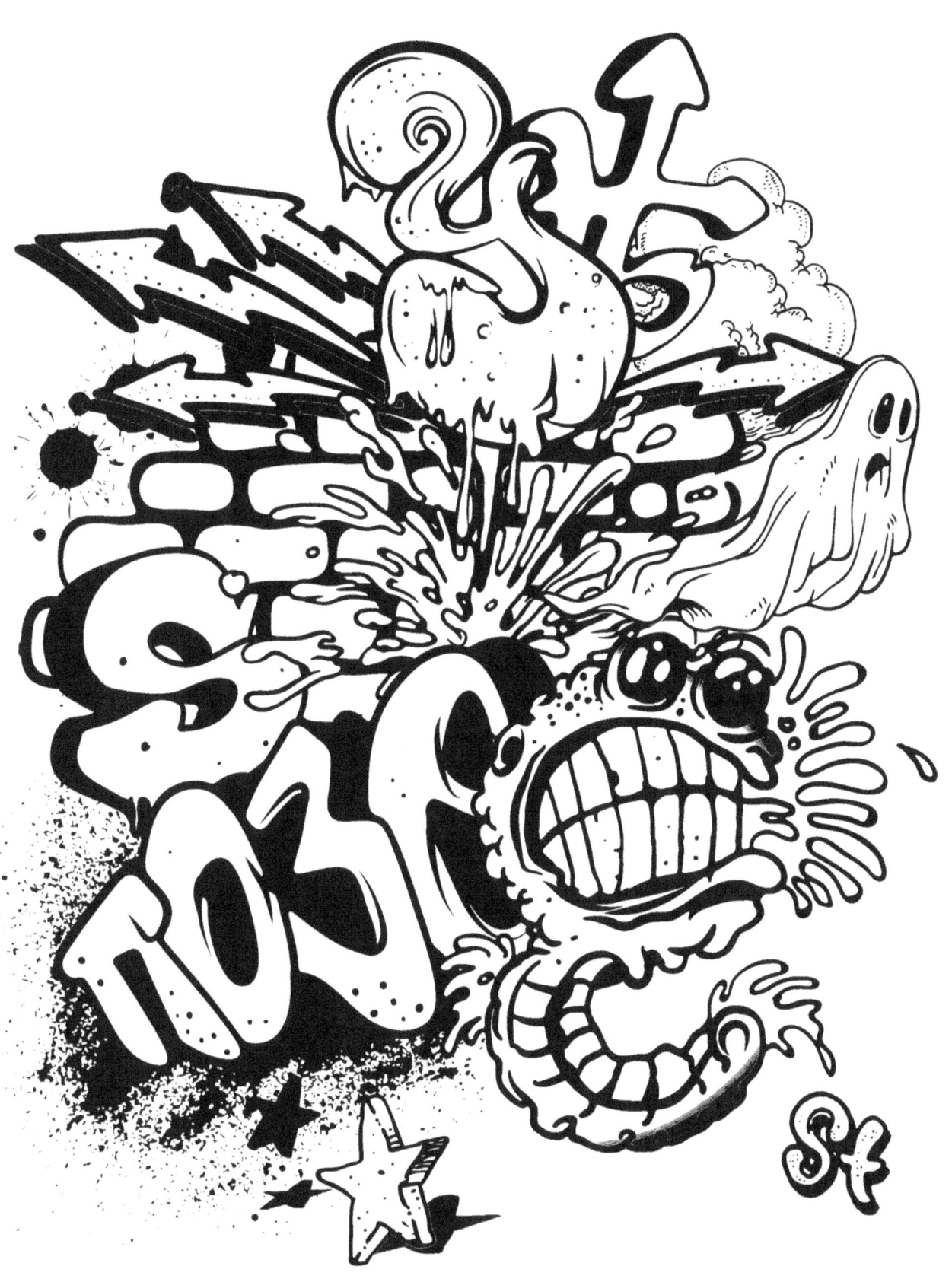

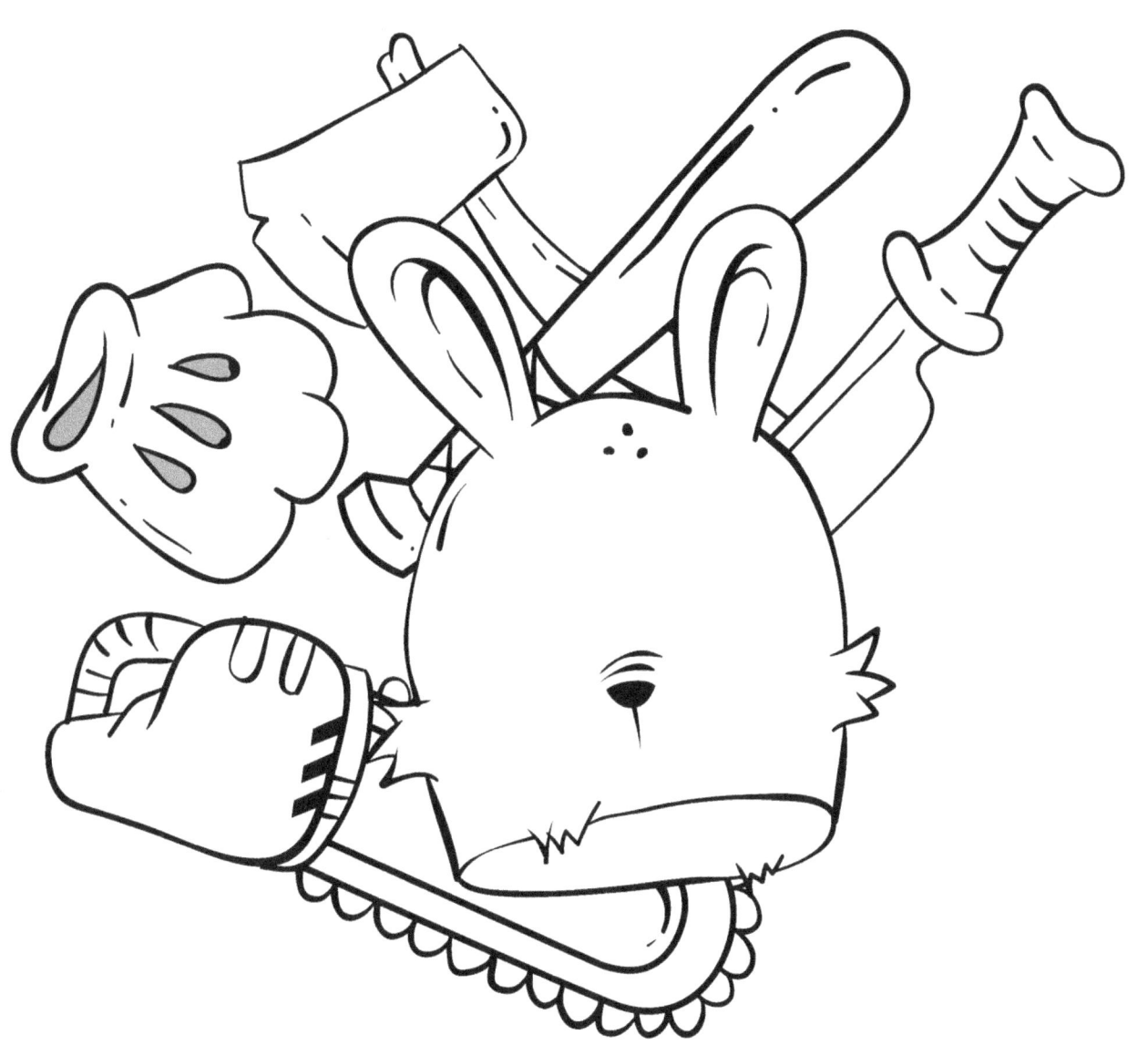

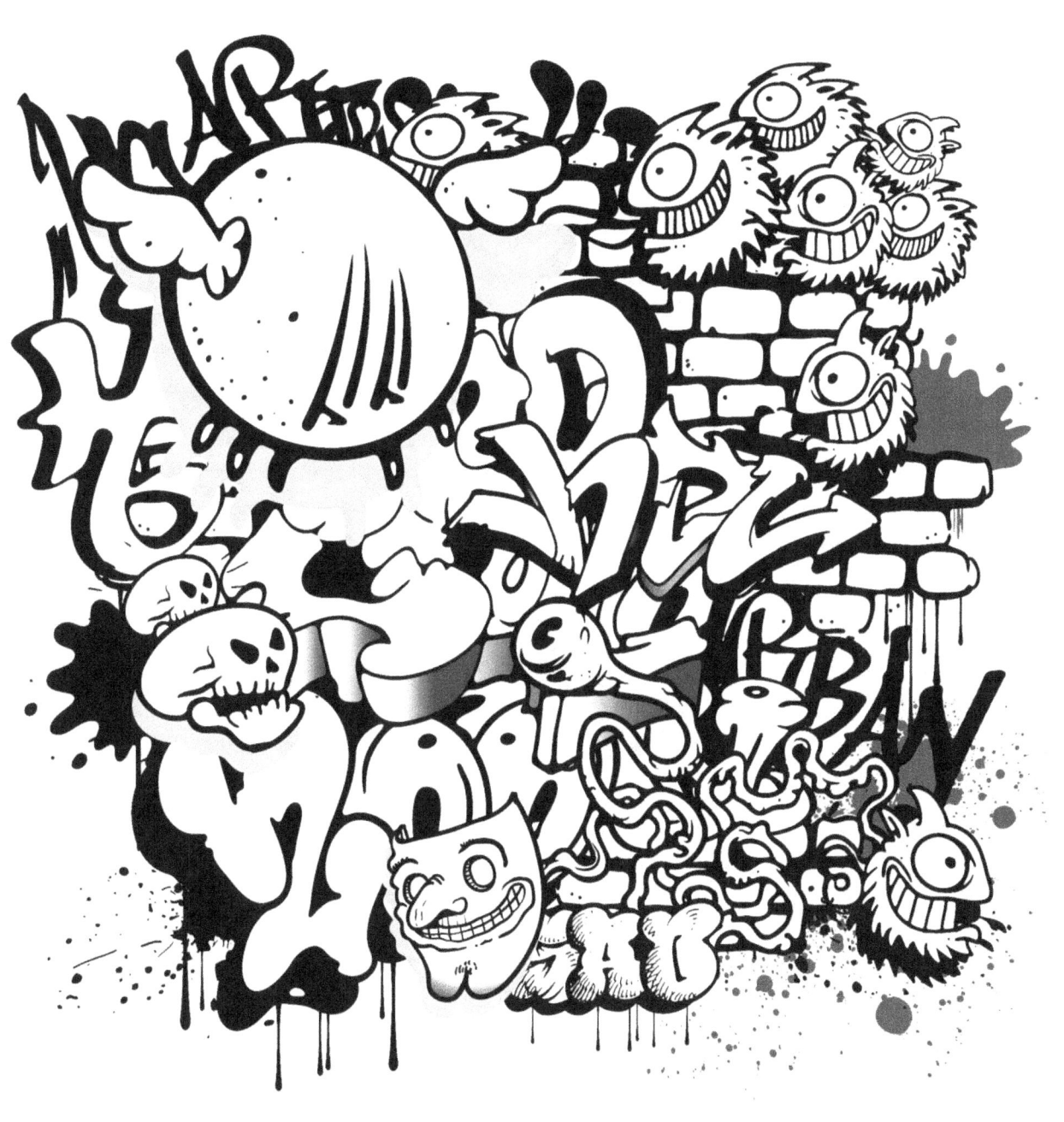

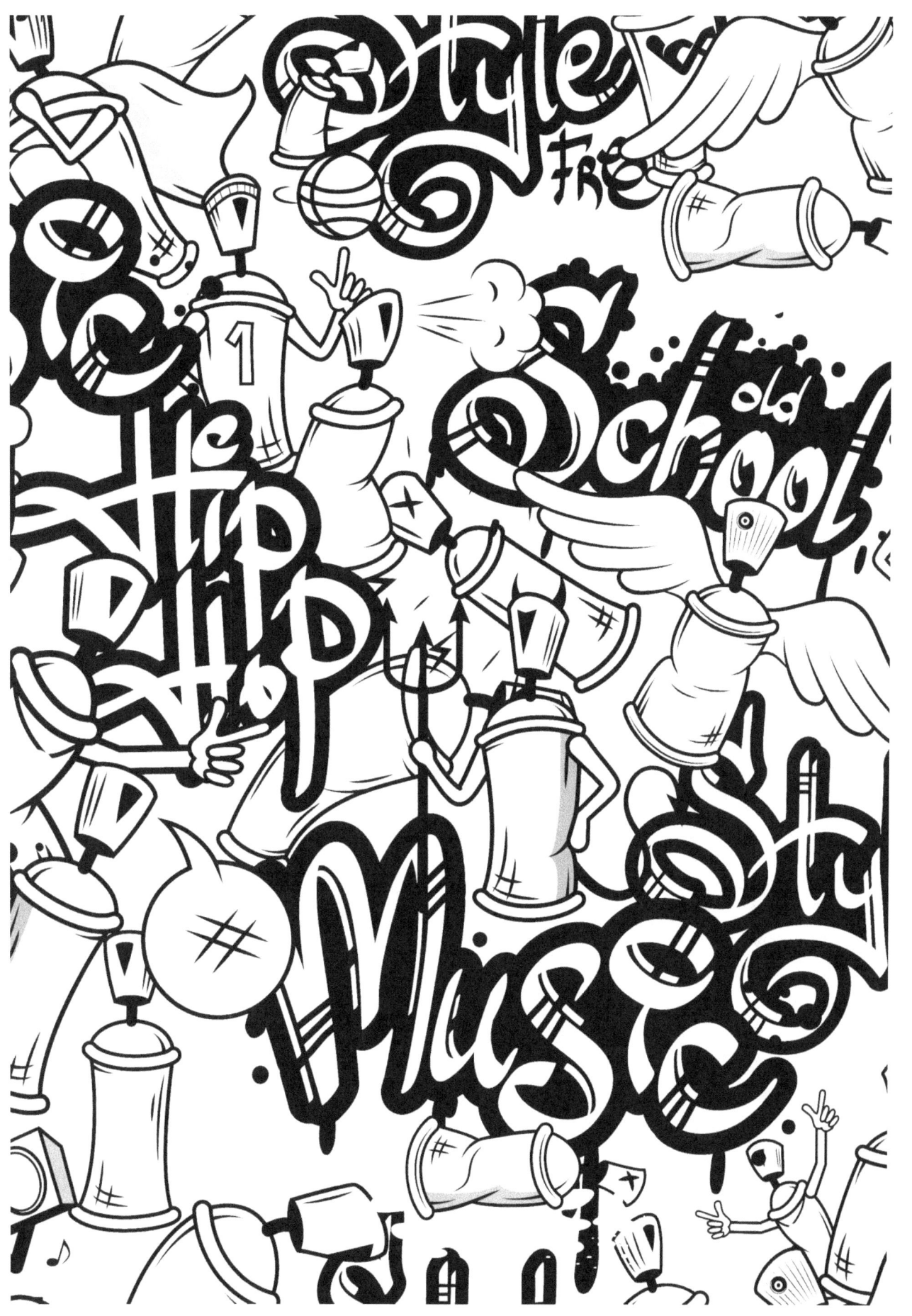

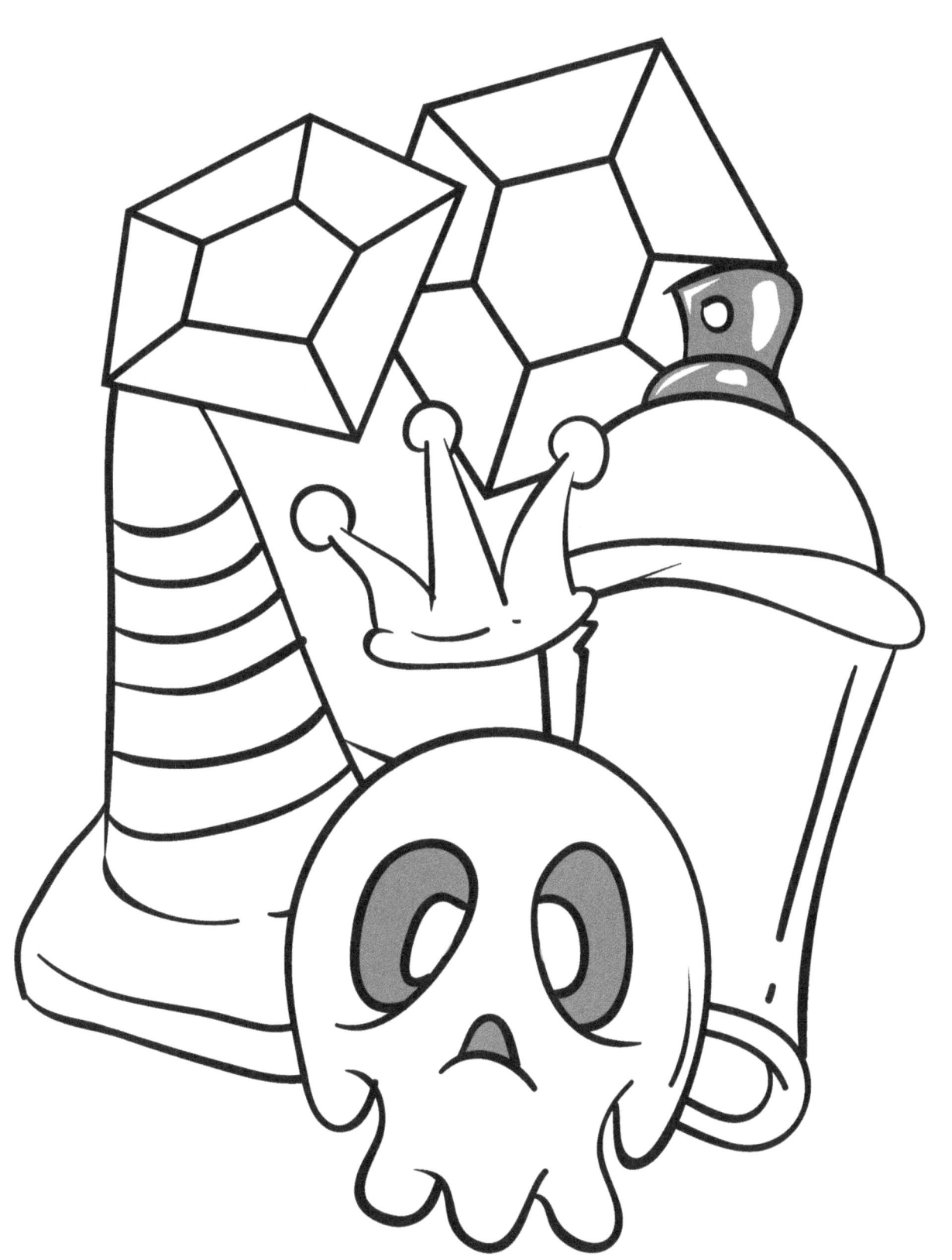

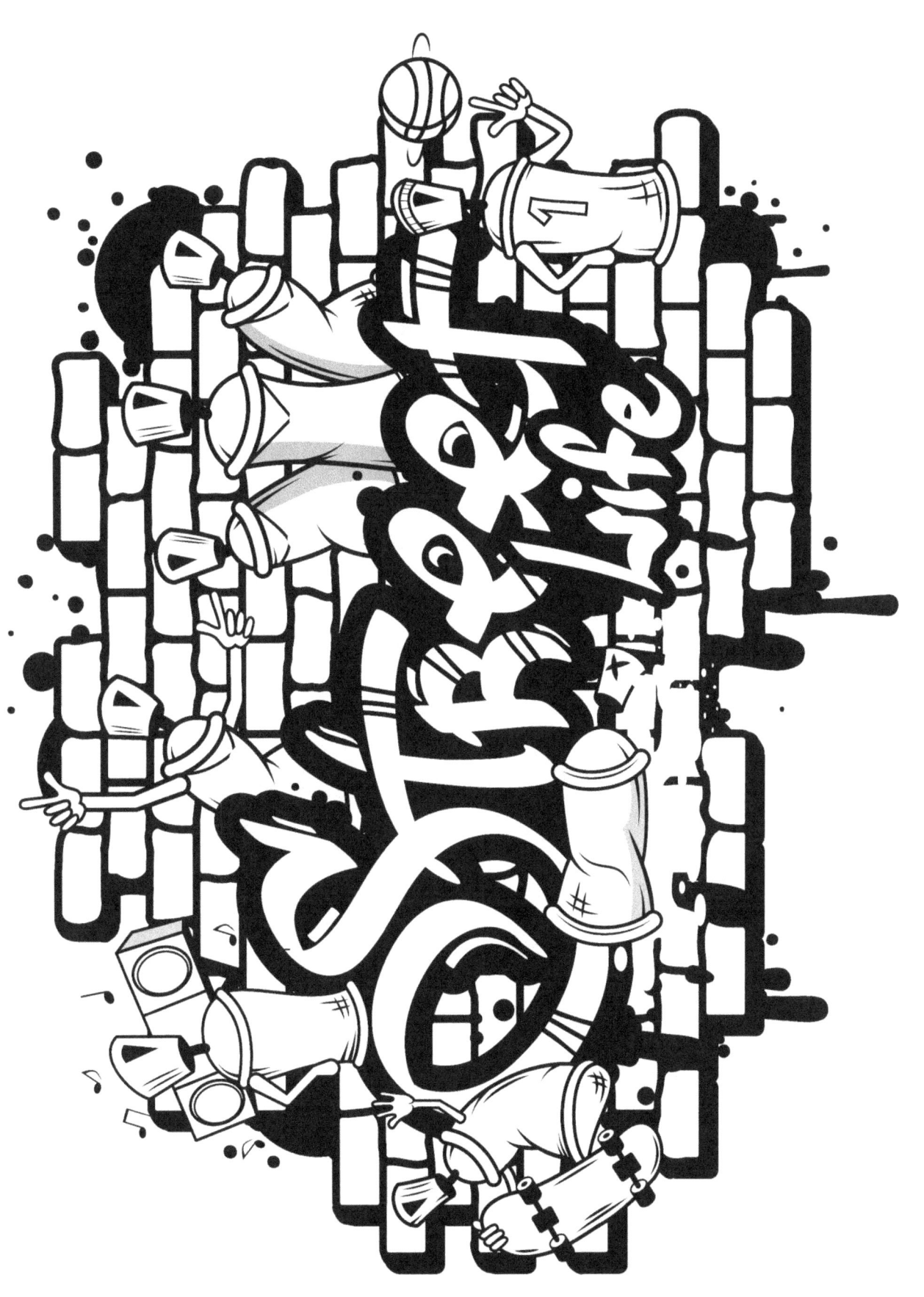

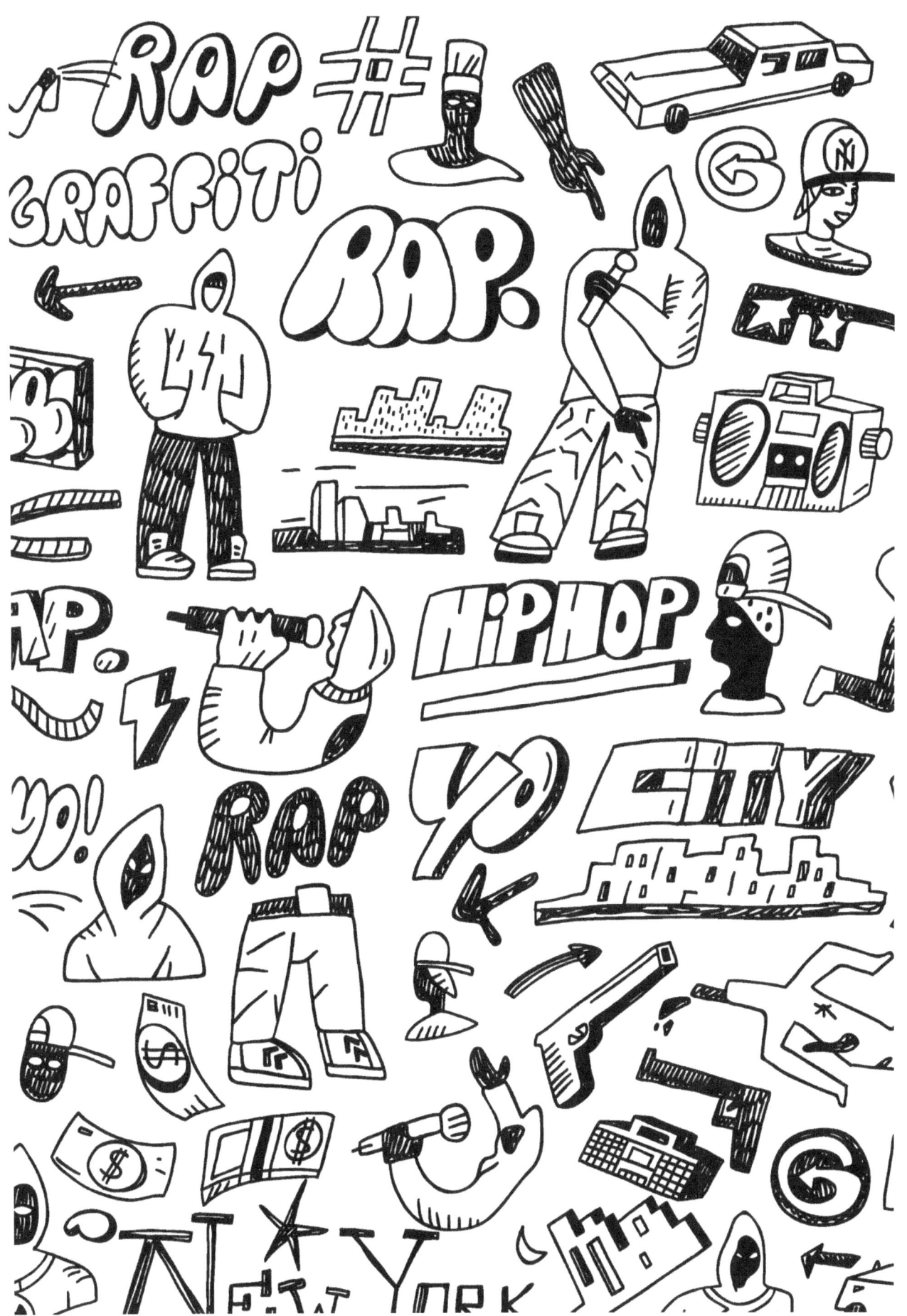

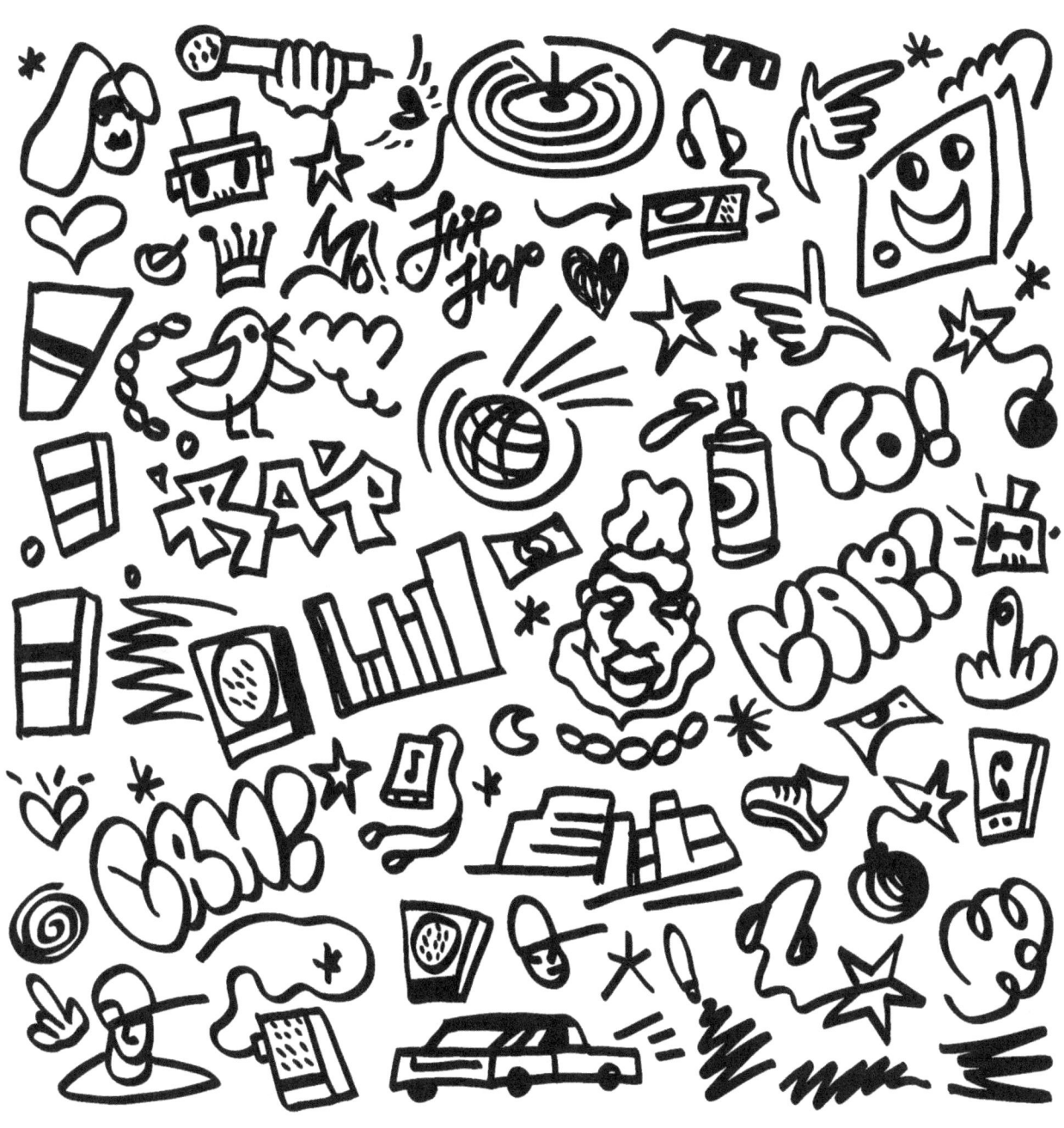

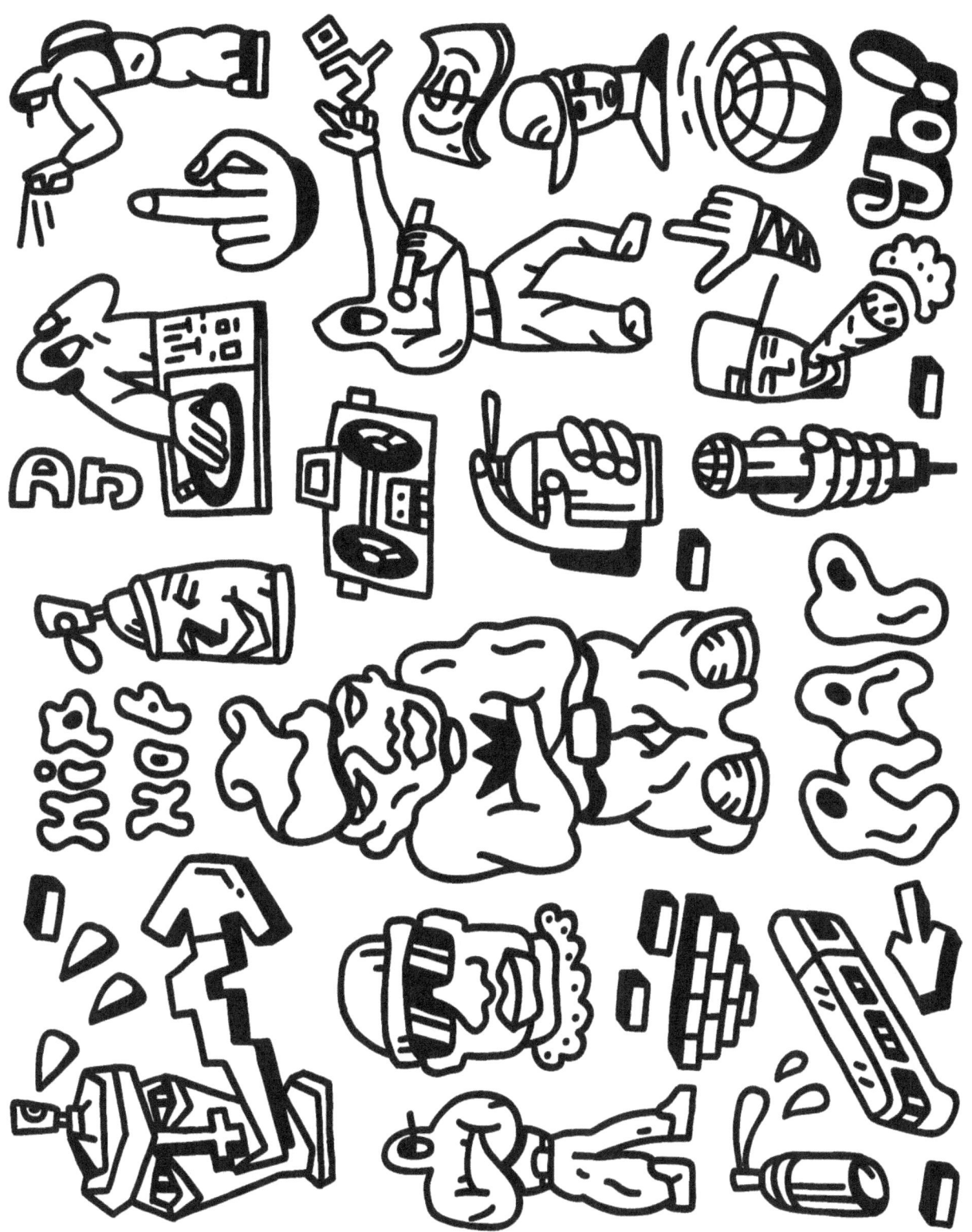

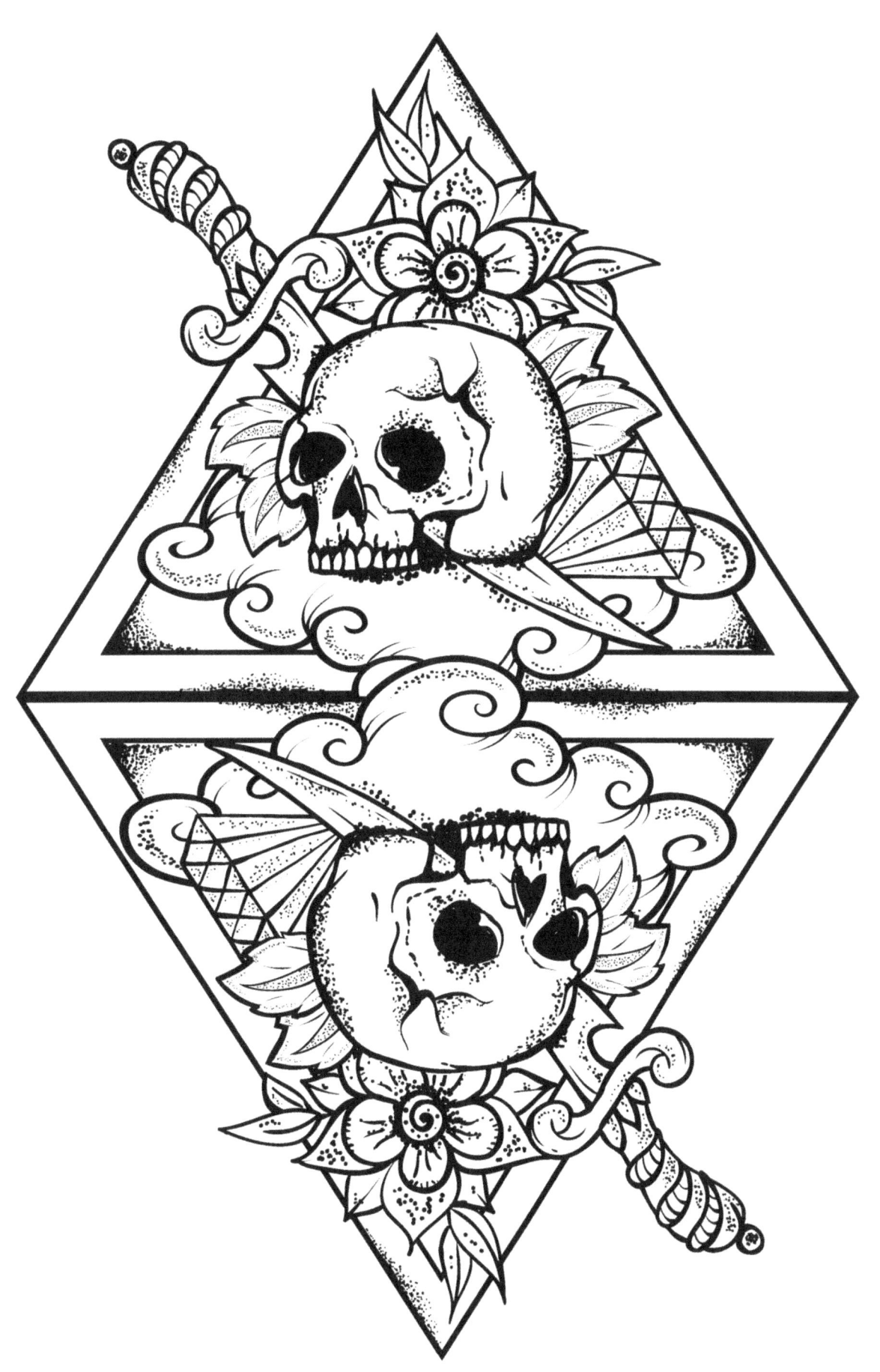

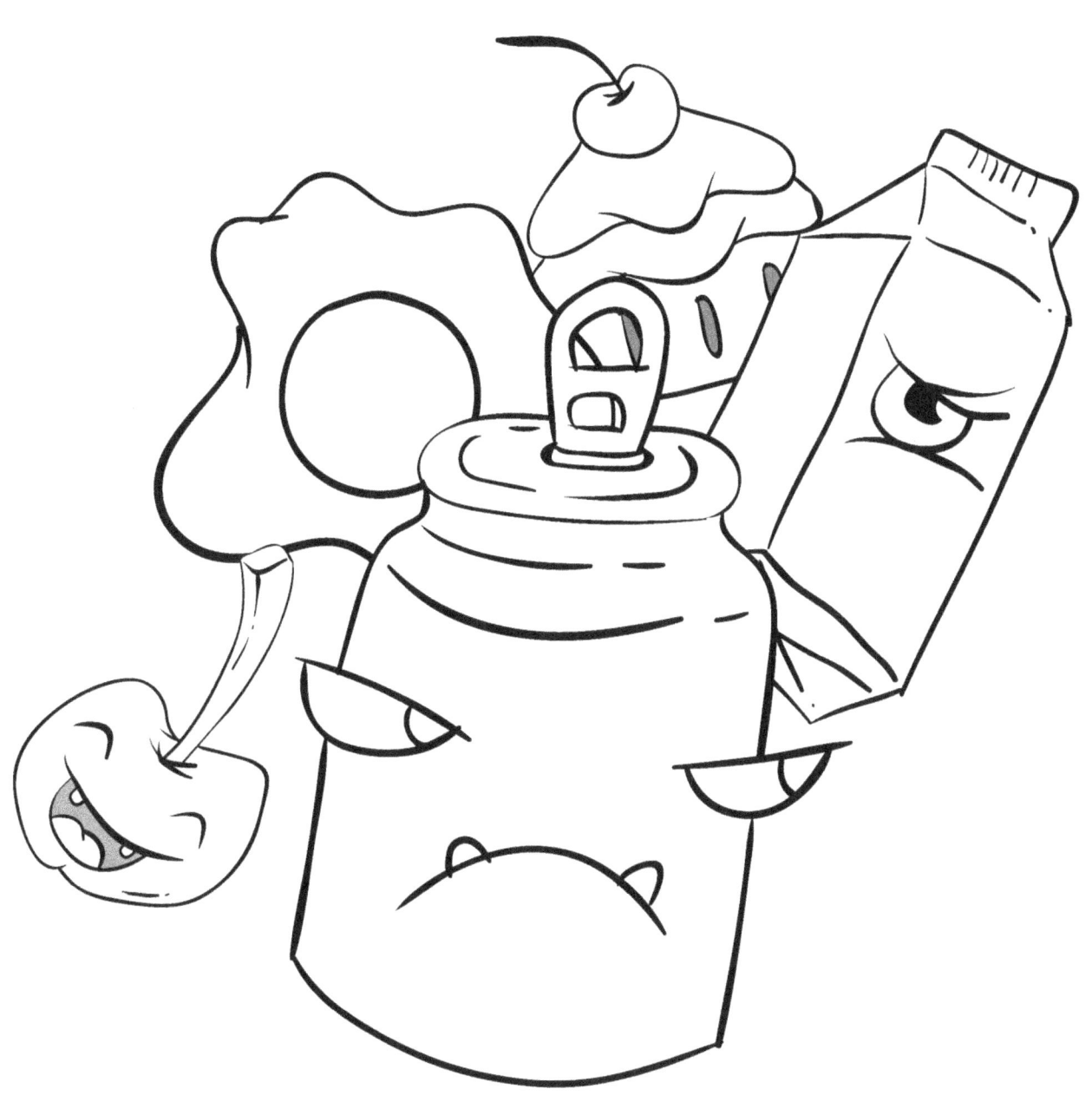

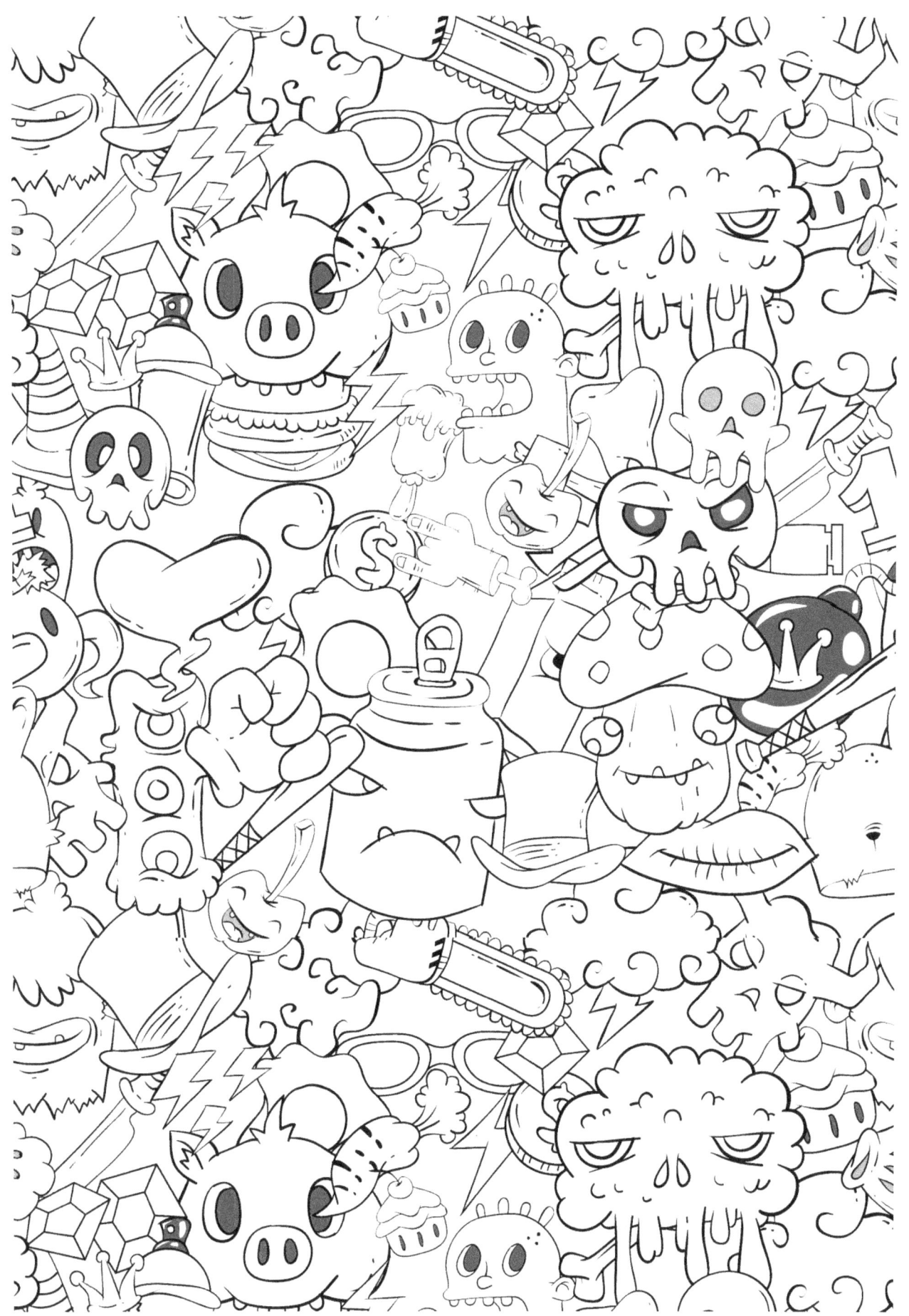

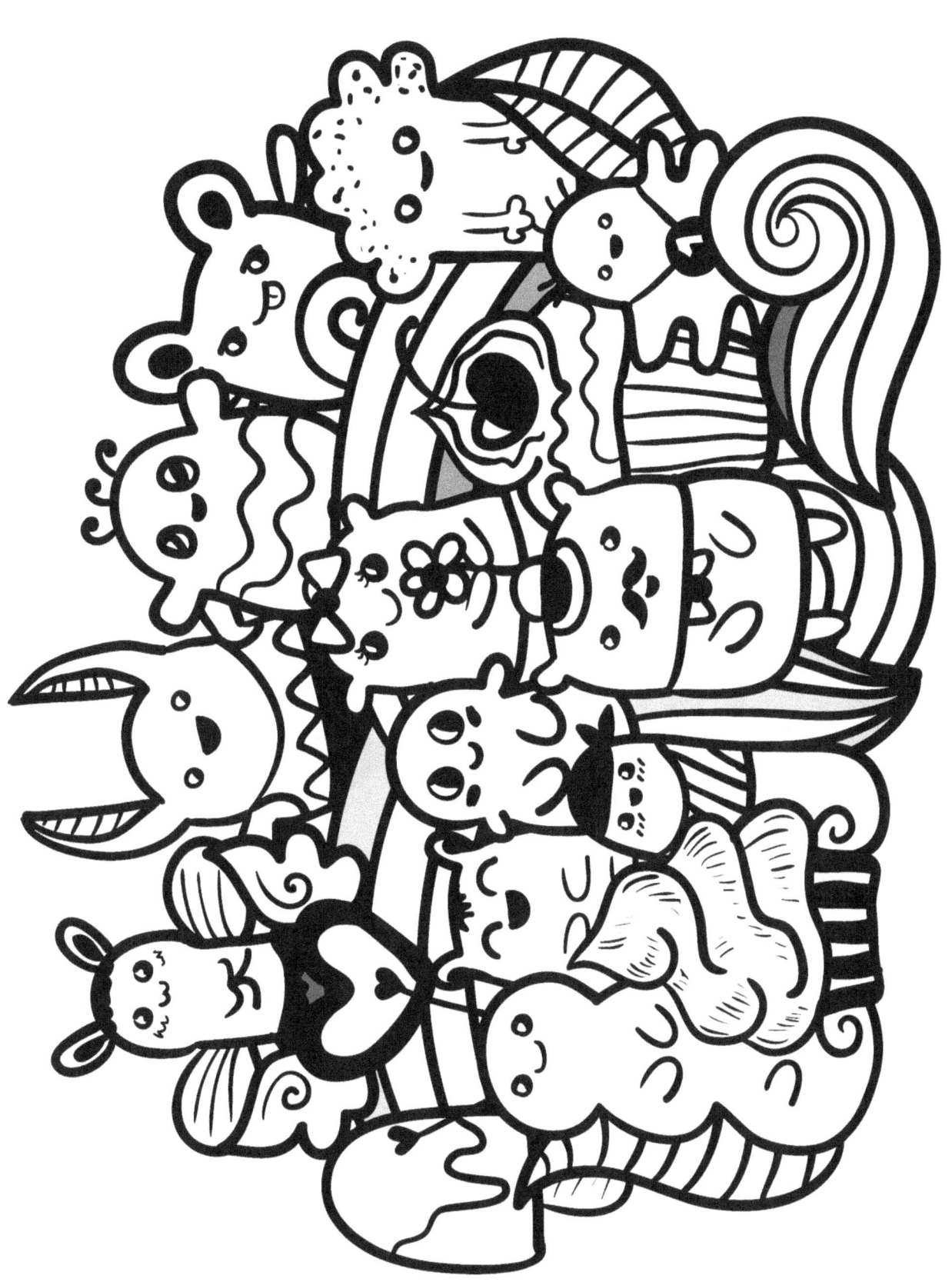

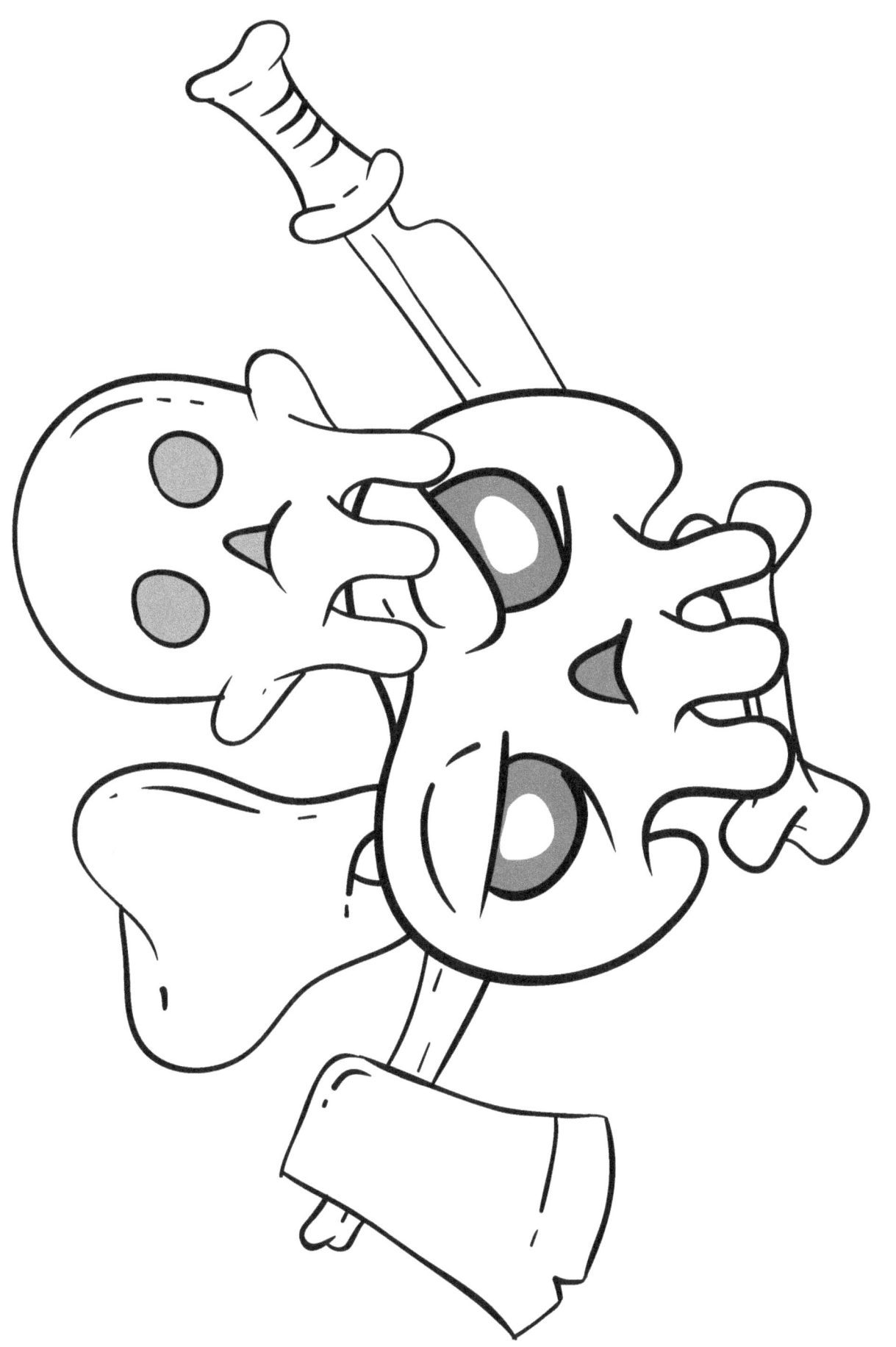

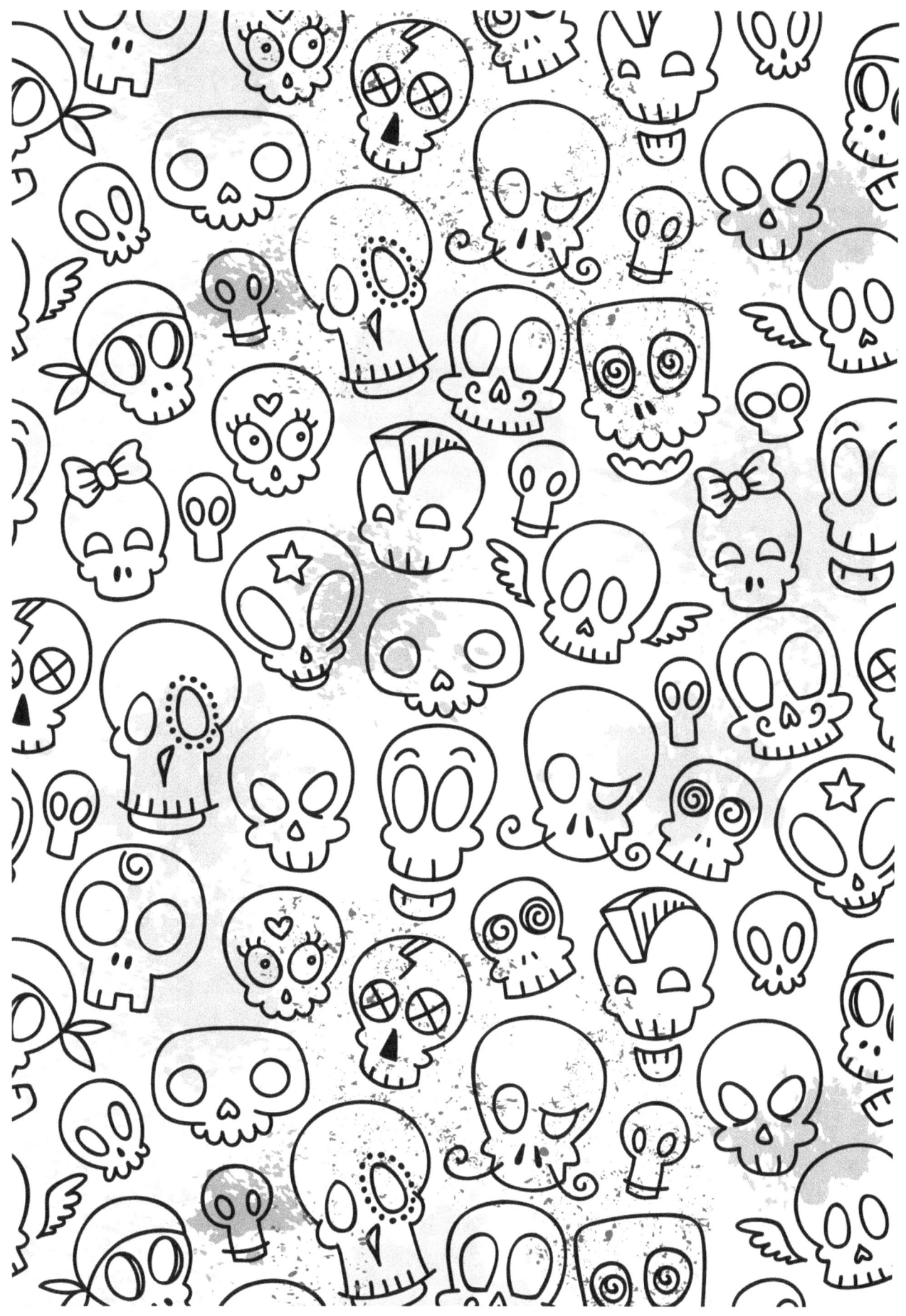

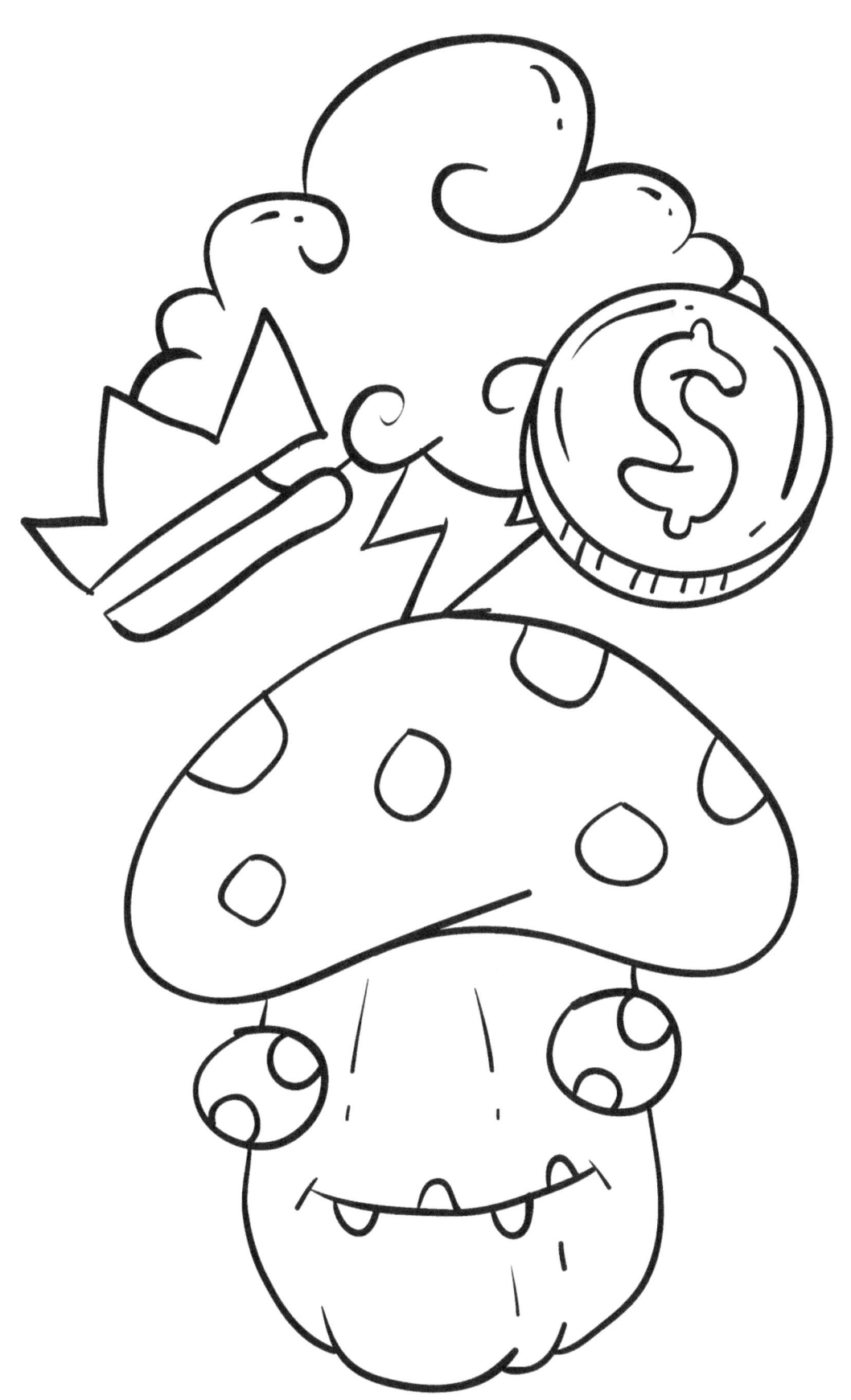

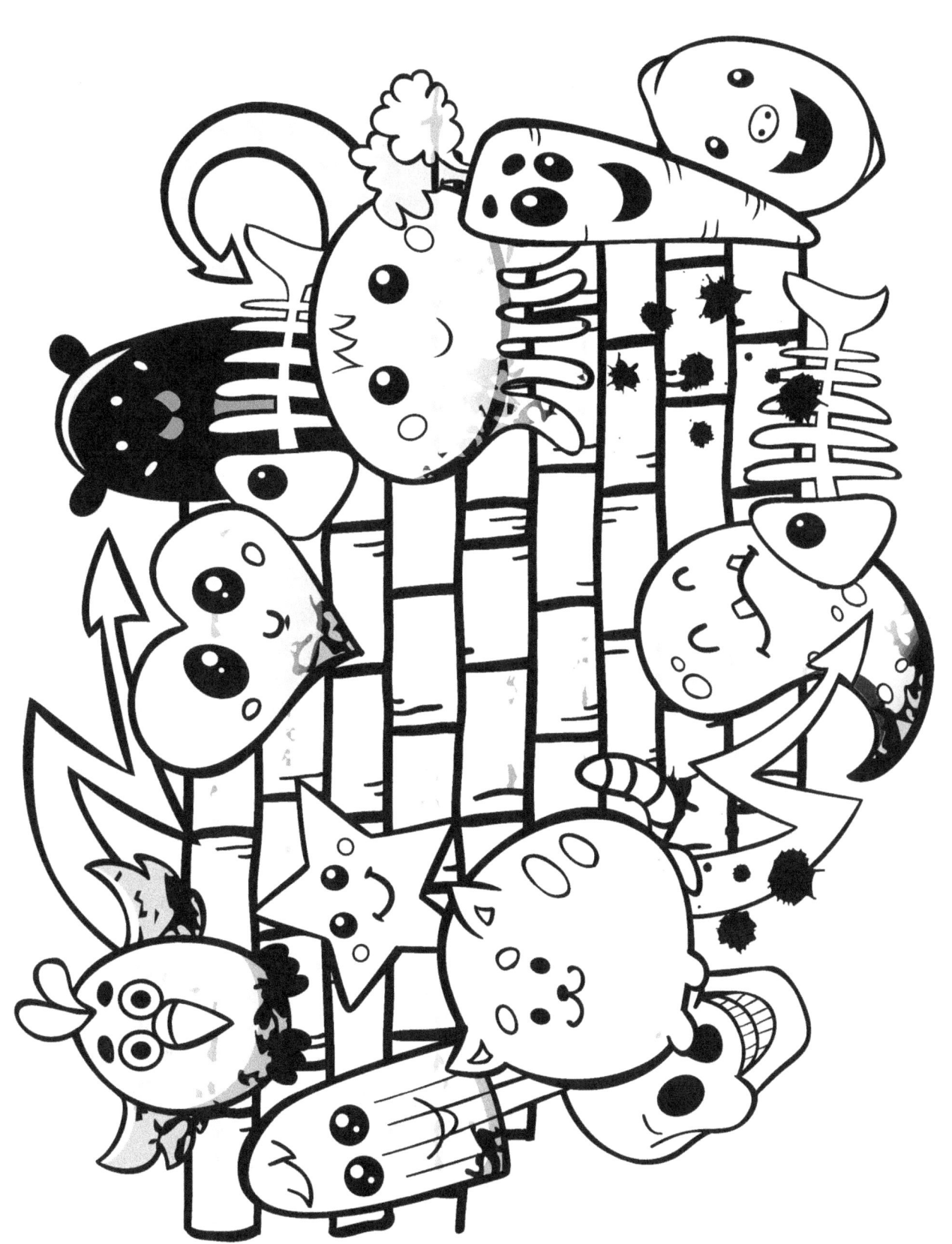

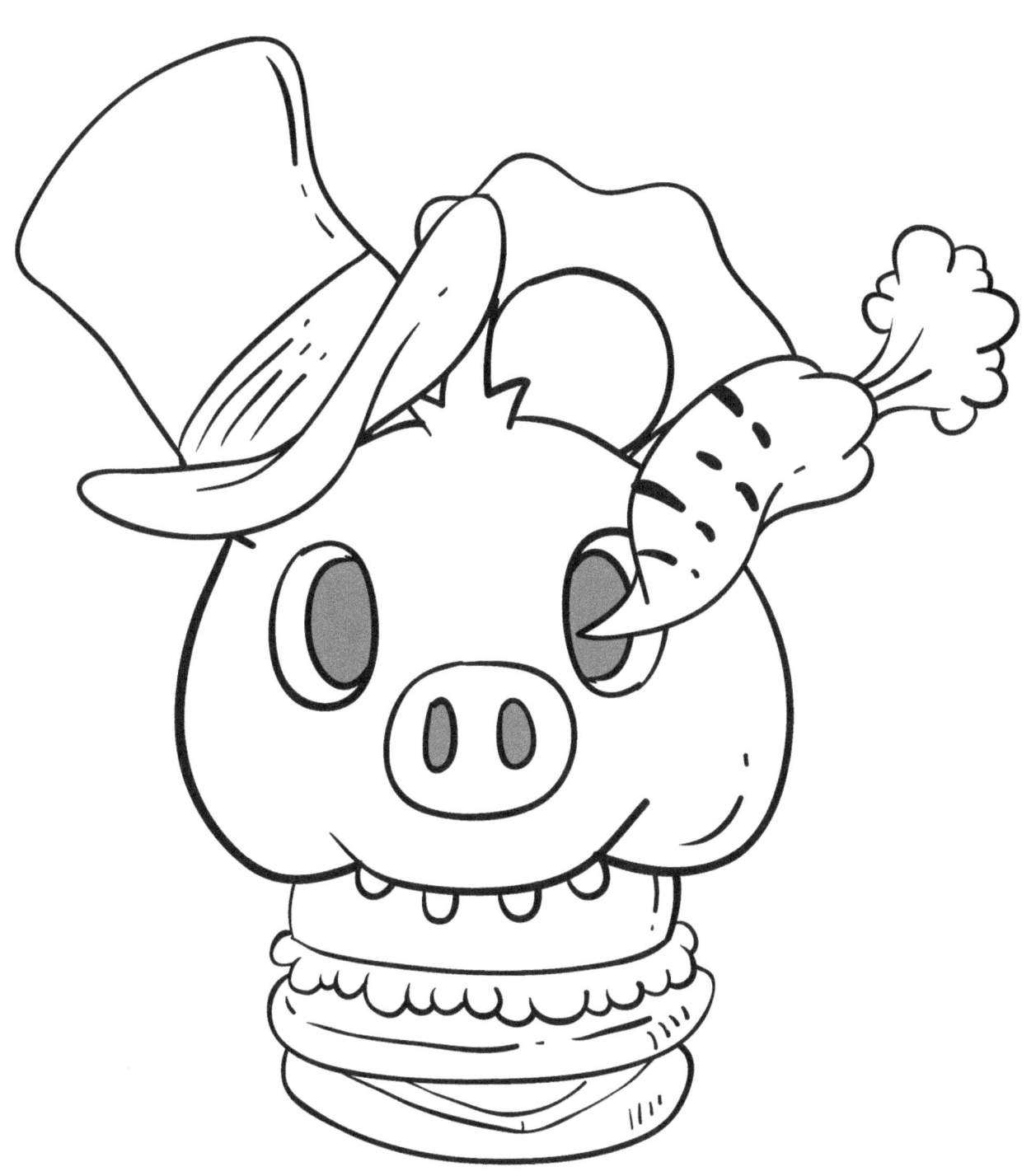

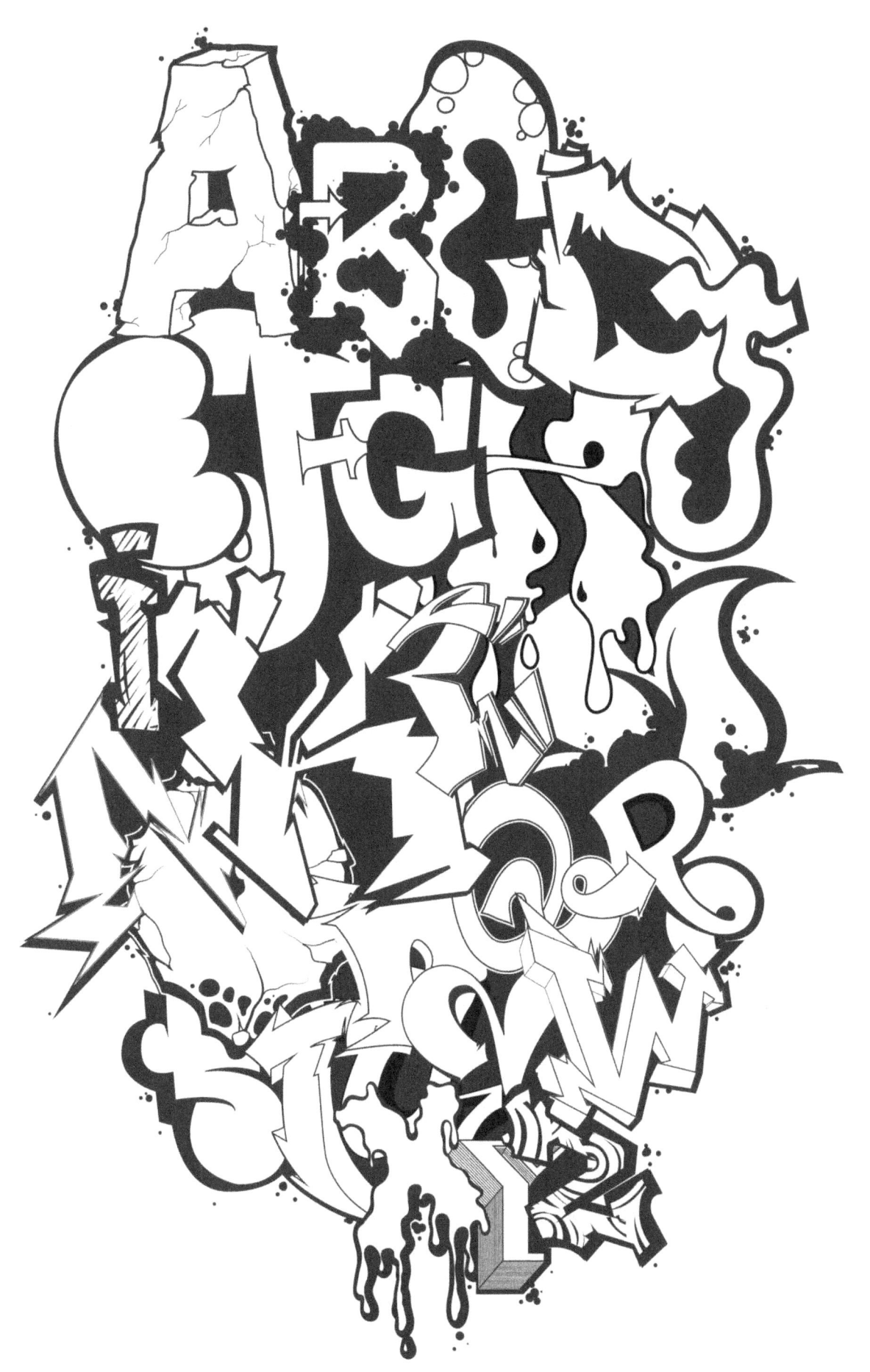

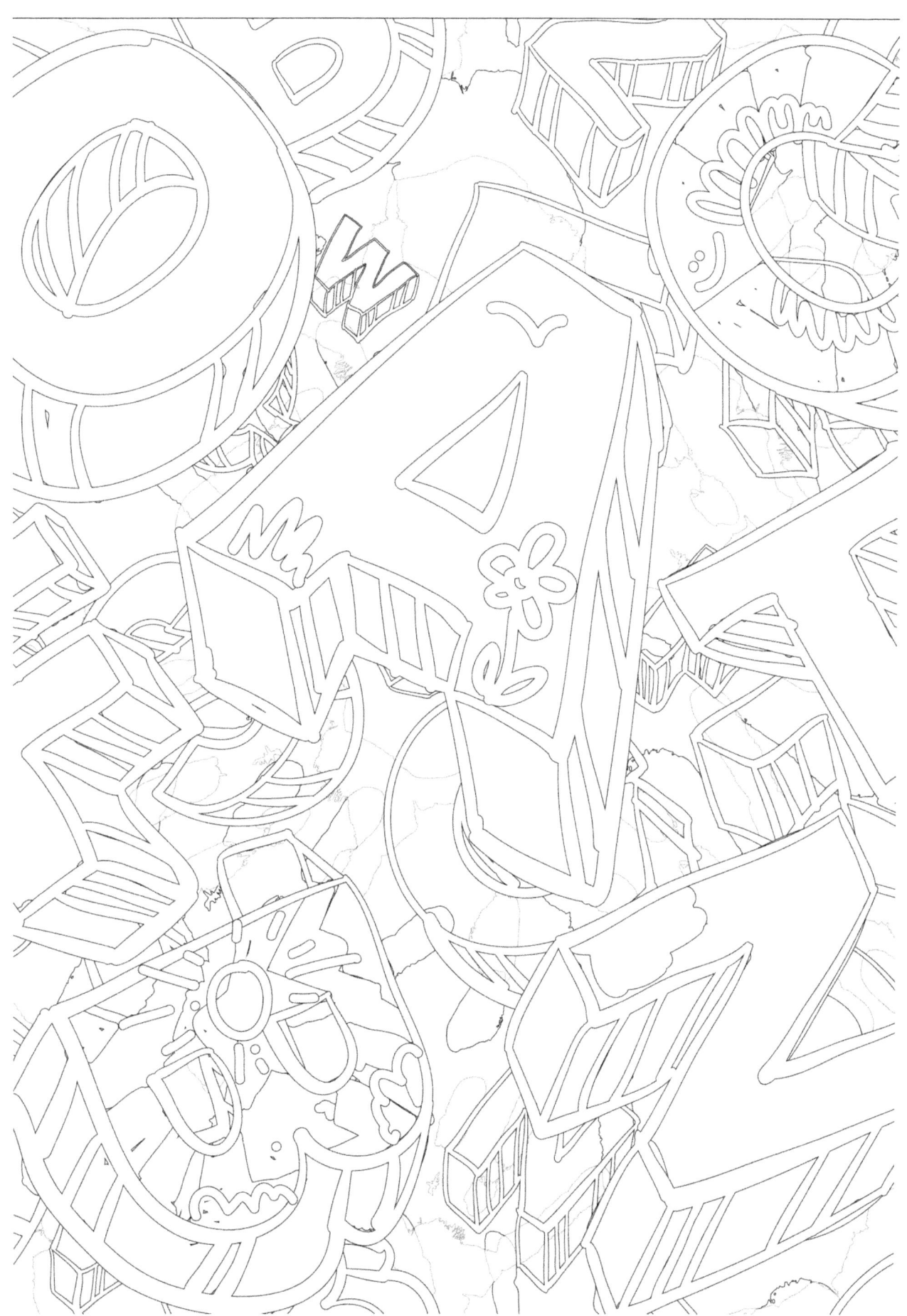

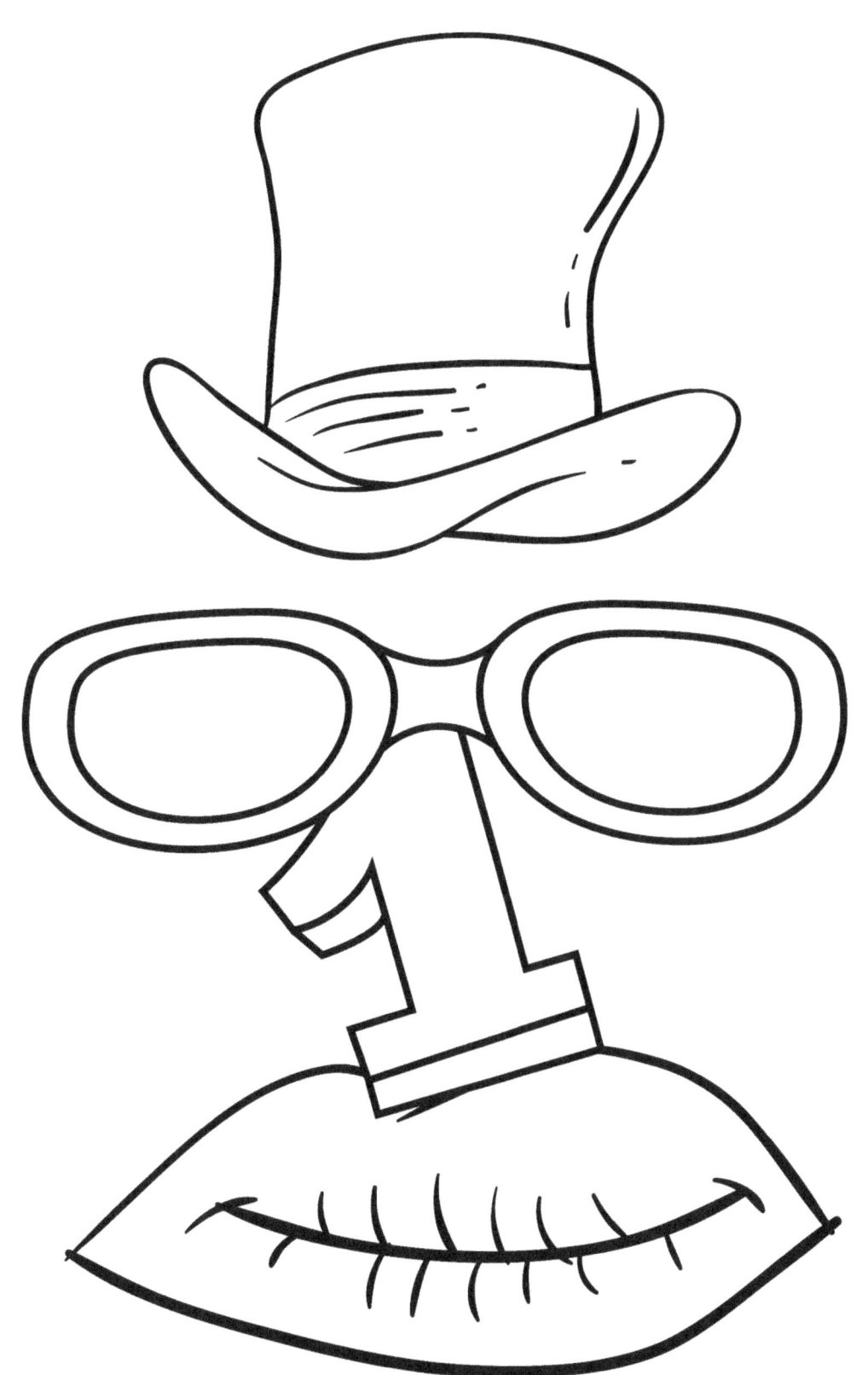

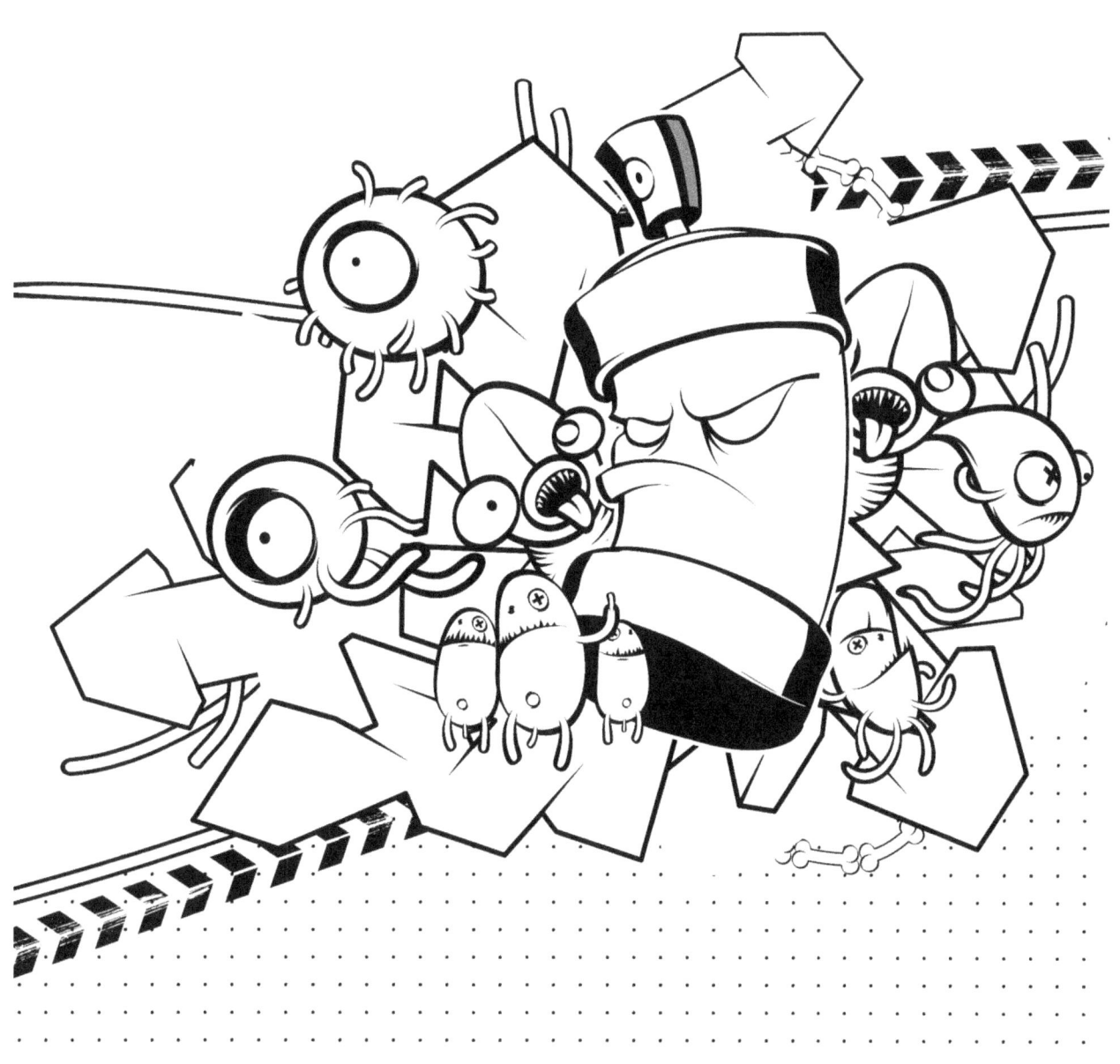

www.ingramcontent.com/pod-product-compliance
Lightning Source LLC
Chambersburg PA
CBHW081248180526
45170CB00007B/2342